COMPANION TO THE POOR

COMPANION TO THE POOR
CHRIST IN THE URBAN SLUMS

VIV GRIGG

Published in partnership with World Vision Resources

Revised and updated edition 2004 by Authentic Media
Revised edition 1990 by Marc Publications
First edition 1984 by Albatross Books and Lion Publishing

09 08 07 06 05 04   10 9 8 7 6 5 4 3 2 1
ISBN 1-932805-13-3

Published by Authentic Media
129 Mobilization Drive, Waynesboro, GA 30830, USA authenticusa@stl.org
and 9 Holdom Avenue, Bletchley, Milton Keynes, Bucks, MK1 1QR, UK

Published in partnership with World Vision
34834 Weyerhauser Way South, P.O. Box 9716, Federal Way, WA 98063 USA
www.worldvision.org

Cover design by Paul Lewis

Printed in the United States of America

Go to the people,
Live among them.
Learn from them.
Start with what they know.
Build on what they have:
But of the best of leaders,
When their task is accomplished,
Their work is done,
The people all remark
'We have done it ourselves.'

Old Chinese Poem

Contents

Foreword

Viv Grigg, author of this book, is in my estimation a modern-day prophet, a special person raised up by God to call his people away from their soft and often ineffective ways of service to new and more courageous paths of ministry.

I have seen the Manila slum where Viv Grigg lived and worked. I have talked with Filipinos about the effect of his ministry on the people in the slum community. I know too the slums of India where the Grigg family now labors. So I know this writer is real. His deeds make his writing both credible and compelling.

Grigg points us to that part of the world's population most in need and in many cases most receptive to the gospel of Jesus Christ: Two-Thirds World[1] urban slum dwellers. He spells out a soundly biblical strategy for urban ministry which involves missionary presence among the slum dwellers, a strong proclamation of the gospel in terms the poor understand, the planting of churches, the social transformation of slum communities through appropriate development techniques, and the reorientation of beliefs and values according to God's Word.

Woven throughout the book is a challenge to middle-class Christians to rethink their lifestyles and priorities. We have to die to ourselves, argues Grigg, in order to live glorious economic resurrection lives for others. At that point, of course, resistance can be expected. Effective, Christlike ministry among the poor seems to many to cost too much.

The power-based Western church enjoys its wealth and privilege, and the mission programs it supports in most cases protect their workers from full identification with the poor and powerless. Here our weakness is uncovered. It lies at the very point where we think we are strong. Our resources, education, and success work against us when they inhibit our ability to carry out Christ's mandate. Grigg challenges us to reexamine our strategies and design new approaches that will build Christ's kingdom among the poor who comprise nearly half the world.

In two areas particularly I find that this book breaks new ground as a training manual for urban missionaries. These have to do with confronting demonic spirits, and social and structural evil. Grigg speaks from his personal experience of living and working among slum dwellers. Along with his neighbors he has felt, even trembled, before raw displays of the powers of darkness. He suggests biblical approaches to both these forms of oppression, not as an uninvolved theoretician but as a pastor and companion to the poor and oppressed.

Some readers may be startled by what he says about the existence and power of demons and the unjust social structures that keep people poor. Missionaries reared in middle-class evangelical churches and trained in Western colleges and seminaries seldom are prepared to deal with these powerful realities. But no one can stay long in the slums of a large city without recognizing that Satan and his representatives are menacingly real. A people's only hope for victory over them lies in Christ and his word.

How to become, through our lives and our engagement in evangelism and community ministries, a transforming influence in the cities, neighborhoods, and nations of the world—that is the burning question before Christ's people. The answer, I think, lies in a commitment to a more radical kind of discipleship that makes following Jesus more life-encompassing and much less comfortable than we have known in the past.

Companion to the Poor projects a vision of what it means to introduce the kingdom of the Lord Jesus among the slum dwellers of an Asian city. It is by holistic evangelism combining presence, proclamation, church planting, and community development that the vision is pursued and to the extent possible before Christ's return, achieved. I believe this is the way God would have us go in a world where so many are materially poor and spiritually lost.

Besides a model of mission strategy, here is an honest and revealing journal of one person's discipleship, a kind of urban *Pilgrim's Progress* with a missionary purpose and kingdom goals. Is not this precisely what the Christian life is all about? Is not this what it means to follow Jesus?

In every place and generation the gospel comes to people living in particular contexts and leads them to ministry among the poor and the lost, and the power of the gospel leads to transformation in all areas of life. Before that transformation can happen in others it must happen in us, which means that the most compelling mission literature will always unite reflection on divine truth with the pilgrim's journal of ministry, struggle, and discovery. Such books cannot be ignored, and such a book is this.

Roger S. Greenway

Notes
1. In the search for a non-derogatory term, the *Third World* became know as the *Two-Thirds World*, indicating its numeric size. This was preferred to *Developing World* which presumes that progressions towards the way the West lives are positive.

Introduction

People who write books usually write about successes. This book is not the story of a success, but of a search and a struggle—a search for the intimate knowledge of a hidden God, whom having found, we yet seek; a struggle to break out of culturally-bound discipleship into a vision for discipling the millions of urban poor in Asia.

Prophets not only dream dreams. They have an inner compulsion to act out symbolically their prophecies. Their lives become cameos of truth, frescoes painted across the wall of grotesque evil. The cameos then become written parables.

This story is such a compulsive cameo, tooled into the darkest places of Asia: the unwanted, ignored, illegal slums of its great cities.

I did not want to write a book aimed at the theoretically-minded, for the God I know is not a teaching, book-writing theologian. He is a God of action whose thoughts and words cannot be divorced from his involvement in history.

This God of active justice, active power, and active compassion walked into the midst of poverty as a fragile, vulnerable Son. And he wants to return—not once but a hundred times—in the lives of other faltering sons and daughters who will confront the demons of poverty face-to-face in the name of the Lord of hosts.

Asia's slum people are poor largely because of injustice and oppression. This book is the story of a rich Westerner trying to understand discipleship in the context of such injustice, poverty, and corruption—incidentally, the social context of most of the Scriptures.

I wrote this during a revival that swelled and captured the majority of the churches of New Zealand, the country of my birth. Out of this revival, mission is springing. The question in the minds of many Christian leaders is, Will this thrust be captured for effective ministry? Hundreds of young people have been stirred.

This book is written with the desire to involve such men and women in long-term, productive mission to Asia's slums. Already, God has raised up a first wave of laborers committed to lifestyles of voluntary simplicity and practical ministry to the poor. May these pages motivate a second wave to other cities of Asia and new structures for mission to the poor. May it also challenge the leaders of existing missions to refocus on an area of need—millions in the great urban mega-cities who have gone without the Word of God.

Gene Tabor, Boni Arzadon, and the REACH staff have provided the stimulus behind many of these ideas—and initially gave me the opportunity and cultural training to pioneer this work. Jun and Milleth Paragas have been special friends who have stood their ground to carry out the ministry at no little cost in reputation, health, and status.

Others have influenced these ideas: Andrew Murray and "Keswick" theology provided the basis of my early experiences of God; Warren Mason taught the mechanics of discipleship and ministry; Gene and Mary Denler graciously drew me into missionary life; Chuck Hufstetler gave hours of his life to mold me into a church-planter; John Waterhouse dared to establish Albatross, a publishing company at the edge of theological thought, and revised much of the manuscript for the first edition; my elders at Hillsborough Baptist, Bob and Prue Wakelin, and Peter and Jenny Vos all gave me the time and quiet places to write. Thanks are due to Sarah Furniss who critiqued the manuscript and Shirley Clarke for her frequent retyping.

While the story is essentially unchanged, a number of names, dates, and places have been changed for the sake of anonymity.

Viv Grigg

Chapter One

City of Contrasts

THE CONFIRMING OF A CALL

I stepped over a mud puddle, ducked beneath a clothesline, and glimpsed the polluted river that surrounds the slums of Tatalon on three sides. I had searched, confused, for fifteen minutes among the labyrinth of concrete block and plywood houses before I saw the line of red, green, and blue buckets leading to the hand pump. I stepped through a small gate to find people standing around, awaiting their turn, and enjoying the early morning sun.

Two girls in patched dresses, their black hair bright and neatly combed, sat on their haunches, washing clothes in large aluminum basins. One looked up to see my fair skin and beard.

"*Si Jesus!*" (It's Jesus!) she exclaimed in Tagalog, the language of Manila, nudging her companion alongside her.

"*Hindi, kaibigan ko lang siya!*" (No, he's just my friend!) I replied, laughing.

I put my bucket hesitantly at the end of the line. With Filipino hospitality, they motioned me—a stranger and a white person—to the front of the line. One of the men worked the long handle up and down for me with great gusto. Since it was my first time at the pump, I accepted the offer of help.

"*Saan po kayo galing?*" (Where have you come from, sir?) the girls asked, still giggling.

"I am living in Aling Nena's upstairs room."

"Why do you want to live *there*?"

I smiled. "A few years ago I learned that Jesus said, 'Blessed are you poor.' I wanted to find out why the poor are blessed."

There were nods and smiles of agreement, so I went on, "I read too that Jesus came to preach the gospel to the poor. I want to preach the gospel to the poor, also."

There were more nods and smiles. We talked and joked until my bucket was full. Sloshing water over my feet, I searched again for the paths back to my rented quarter of a squatter home.

Children looked at me shyly as I walked by. At Aling Nena's home, I climbed the three steps up the eight-foot vertical ladder to my room. More water sloshed down the ladder. I put my bucket down with a sigh of relief and sat on a bench in the room. It was a good place to sit and look out over my newfound community.

I thought back to the night before.

A typhoon had come with the fury of the gods. The rain of sleet and the sound of crackling thunder seemed like a final demonic onslaught to prevent me from carrying my few belongings into the house. I had been battling a bout of fever all day, and none of my friends had been free or willing to brave the typhoon to help.

I had returned the jeep and retraced the way to my new home by public transport in the dead of night. My first night as a squatter of Tatalon was the culmination of years of dreaming and preparation—and I was dizzy, weary, and sick. It was as if all the forces of oppression were thrown against me in my effort to live among the slum dwellers of Manila.

But I knew God wanted me there. Even this room was a sign of his faithfulness.

Three weeks ago, I had written this prayer in my diary: "Lord, find me two rooms in Tatalon's slum area with cooking facilities and adequate sewerage. They need to be upstairs so that I might have a quiet place for prayer and study, and with windows to allow for a cooling breeze—before September the third."

On September first, I was talking to Aling Nena in her home. (*Aling*, meaning "older lady," is perhaps equivalent to the English

"Mrs." and followed by a person's first name.) I'd heard she had a room available. Embarrassed at the poverty of her empty upstairs room, she made an adjoining room available for me as well. Her niece could move downstairs.

I knew this was the answer to my prayer: a quieter, upstairs room for myself, an adjoining room for companions, and a small kitchen space—quite a kingly situation for a squatter.

An answer to prayer in a long series of answered prayers. Twenty years earlier, with the intensity of a vision, I had seen my destiny stretched out before me. It was a call directly from my Maker: to live among these people of the slums, to preach the gospel to the poor. As I looked back on the journey that had brought me to Tatalon, even with the storm raging outside and my fever raging within, I knew I was home.

I had replaced the boards that covered the entrance to my room. Finding a match and candle, I sat and took stock of my surroundings. Three windows would give me a breeze and a view overlooking the other homes. Lights flickered in windows throughout the neighborhood like symbols of hope in the midst of the dark oppression that is squatter poverty.

I gave thanks for the guava tree that grew outside my window. In the midst of a treeless expanse of plywood, rusted iron, cardboard, plastic bags, and old tires, the tree would remind me again and again of the goodness of God in the months to come.

Out of the darkness

As I prayed into the dark hours of that first night in Tatalon, I wondered what the next steps would be. *How do you bring a whole city to the light? How can you rescue three million squatters and slum dwellers?*

Suddenly, a beautiful gold and white creature scurried along some smoke-blackened rafters of my new home. It was a well-fed rat, sleek and cunning. I watched silently, intrigued and curious, as he made his way gracefully across the wood, avoiding splinters and knotholes.

The cross of Christ was made of the same rough wood as this squatter home, I thought.

Within the inner recesses of my spirit, God seemed to be speaking—directly, personally:

> Carry my cross. It is an instrument of death. You must die to yourself in order to be a servant of this people.
>
> For unless a grain of wheat falls into the ground and dies, it cannot bear fruit. If it dies, it bears much fruit. This cross commands absolute authority over all people, all history, all cultures.
>
> Preach the cross! In it is the salvation of this people: from drunkenness and despair, from broken families and oppression, from poverty and desolation. In it alone is their hope.
>
> Remember, it is a rugged cross. Do not return to a tinsel cross. Take up my cross and follow in my footsteps, for I too chose poverty.

The next evening, a seven-year-old girl came shyly up the stairs. "Would you join us, sir?" she asked me. "We are saying a novena for Aling Nena's husband."

"What is a novena?"

"We are praying so his spirit does not return to the house and annoy us! He died a year ago now." Later, I would learn that even after this novena, they would pray each year for his spirit to leave and stop troubling them.

I was unsure of the correct response. "May I bring my new Tagalog Bible and read from it?"

We climbed down the ladder, and I stooped into the doorway. About fifteen relatives were kneeling in front of the makeshift altar. An old lady chanted to the saints and icons that were laid out—which included a statue of the Virgin Mary. She was a professional chanter. The others joined in at appropriate times. Candles and other symbolic mementos had been placed neatly on the table.

I sat quietly and listened, trying to understand. At the end, they asked if I would say something. In halting Tagalog, I read the story of the resurrection in 1 Corinthians 15. It was the first "sermon" I had given in my new language. They listened politely in obvious appreciation of my presence as a religious man. A poor, gambling family would have found it difficult to convince a priest to attend.

As they listened reverently to the words of the Bible, I rejoiced. The rugged cross had come to Tatalon!

Afterwards, I stayed for a snack of *pancit* (Chinese noodles), sandwiches, and a cup of coffee, enjoying their laughter and friendship.

Aling Nena had been one of the original squatters in Tatalon. Twenty-five years ago, she had lived right on the banks of the river. As time went on, the first squatters rented out rooms in their homes to newer squatters. This provided a reasonable source of income. Those in the upper quarters of a house usually rented rooms from the owners who lived downstairs.

Aling Nena was one of a clan, an extended family of about forty who lived in several houses in one area. She was also the chief gambler of a gambling den operating under my bedroom.

Aling Nena was deeply honored to have a foreigner and a "man of God" stay in her house. But she did not fully realize the implications of what she had done, as Jesus described them: "He who receives you receives me . . . He who receives a prophet because he is a prophet shall receive a prophet's reward . . . And whoever gives to one of these little ones even a cup of cold water because he is a disciple, truly, I say to you, he shall not lose his reward" (Matthew 10:40–42).

She would be the first in the community to believe. Through Aling Nena, many gamblers heard of the cross of Jesus Christ, and several in her extended family believed.

Metro-Manila

Aling Nena's house in Tatalon was not my first home in Manila. Years earlier, I had stepped off the plane for the first time, the tropical humidity hitting me like a shock wave.

Friends had welcomed me as we drove across the city on an eight-lane highway jammed with cars, buses, and trucks. It took two hours to travel through the twenty miles of towns and cities that ring Manila. Metro-Manila consists of four cities and thirteen towns.

The heat and smell hit me as we crossed the river, the pungent odor overpowering. Fuming buses crazily raced against each other, pouring out enough dirty black smoke to cover a man in half a minute.

We passed by the rich mansions of Makati—the wealthy multinational and banking center. Behind high brick walls, palm trees waved in the breeze. Half-built concrete structures, towering office blocks, gleaming supermarkets, and movie theaters spoke of prosperity and commercial bustle.

The houses decreased in size as we drove through the poorer city of Caloocan and moved down a side road into the town of Valenzuela. Finally, we were out into one of the middle-class subdivisions. A driveway led to a beautiful Spanish-American style mansion behind a concrete and iron-paling fence.

Manila is a mosaic of different cultures. Four hundred years before, the Spanish had conquered this archipelago of 7000 islands scattered in the South China Sea and named it after their reigning monarch, King Philip. The Malay peoples dwelling there were scattered around the islands, speaking over a hundred different dialects. Arab traders had converted many of the settlements (called *barangays* or *barrios*) to Islam. But behind the Spanish sword marched the Spanish cross of Catholicism. Many priests lived heroic and saintly lives for the gospel. Others were leaders in exploiting the people.

In 1898 the Filipinos threw off the Spanish yoke, only to be taken over by the Americans in 1901. Along with educational, medical, and commercial systems, the Americans opened the door for a new wave of missionaries.

The first Filipino believers were stoned to death. At times Bibles were burned. Nevertheless, thousands responded to the gospel, experiencing a new freedom in Christ from the old bondage of animism and Catholicism. At the time of this writing however, 84 percent of the population remained Catholic-animist. The culture and even the modes of speech are deeply influenced by the need to appease or utilize the spirits, the saints, the Virgin Mary, and God himself.

Like other urban centers in Asia, Manila has undergone rapid change. The *barangay* that was an Arab and Chinese trading post became the Spanish Fort Santiago in Manila and later the center of American-Japanese warfare. Today the original center is surrounded by the bustle and laughter of over eight million Metro-Manilans, some enjoying their fortunes in magnificent mansions, others seeking theirs, while yet others trying to eke out a living to overcome perpetual hunger.

One of the cities, Quezon City, is the center of bureaucracy and government for fifty million Filipinos. Manila City itself is a bustle of Chinese businesses, import-export businesses, street-hawkers, and one million students, crammed twelve per room. The density of Metro-Manila today is over 100,000 people per square mile. Thousands of gaily-decorated *jeepneys* (converted World War II jeeps seating seven along each side at the back) move through the main streets, filling the city with fumes and loud music.

Supporting the growth of this steaming mega-city is a highly productive and mineral-rich hinterland, roughly the size of New Zealand. Rice, corn, cassava, sugar, bananas, and pineapple grow readily. The country exports coconut oil, clothing, electrical equipment, metal ores, fruit and vegetables, timber, and sugar. But the forests have been rapidly destroyed, leading to flooding of formerly rich agricultural provinces during the 20 typhoons that ravage the country yearly. Minerals are also rapidly being exploited by the richer nations.

Muslim rebels in the south and a growing New People's Army of Marxist guerillas in a number of provinces pose a constant threat to President Gloria Arroyo.

The country, essentially ruled by 400 rich families, has a gross national product of only US $4,600 per person (compare New Zealand US $20,100; USA US $36,300)[1] The poor are very poor and the rich are very rich.

Yet life expectancy is relatively high (66.44 years for men and 69.44 years for women)[2] due to the American emphasis on medical facilities and some years of stable government. Of the total population, about half are below fifteen years of age. The population of this city has exploded since the war—at a rate of five per cent per year, from 1.7 million in 1950 to 5 million in 1975, 10.9 million in 2000, and an estimated 14.8 million by the year 2015.[3]

Manila is a highly educated society with over one million students in colleges and universities. The country has an overall literacy rate of 88 percent. Practical and technical training are developing rapidly to provide a base of expertise for industrialization.

During the decade of martial law in the seventies, major infrastructure projects in Metro-Manila were completed. There are now concreted highways and effective sewer, water, and telephone systems, giving a sense of progress and development.

But there are areas of horror within the city, particularly in "the tourist belt" with its opulent hotels, brothels, and discos— ironically, in a country once known for its modesty. Manila's rivers are filled with gaseous effluents emanating from thousands of uncontrolled factories. And against the backdrop of a modern city skyline, hundreds of hastily constructed shacks, made up of packing cases and plywood, take up every vacant lot or public place.

Yet even man cannot destroy all of God's beauty. The gold and pink hues of Manila Bay's sunsets continue unabated. Outlying suburbs on rolling hills twenty miles from the center of the city enjoy cooling breezes, the landscape dotted with trees and grass.

Above all, the Filipino soul, with its capacity for adaptation, survives all the traumas of urbanization, relocation, exploitation, and unemployment with a *joie de vivre* and a romantic, poetic optimism. Even the poorest of the poor dream of moving into a bureaucratic job and a middle-class subdivision, hoping that God, friends, fate, Virgin, saints, and spirits will be favorable.

Urbanization

But the extent of urban poverty in Manila is not atypical. Among the specters of poverty, few can match the endless spreading slums and squatter areas of the sprawling Two-Thirds World mega-cities.

Since the industrial revolution, almost every major city has had its share of squatters and slum dwellers. Earlier this century, when European cities were growing, nations were able to cope with this problem through increased exploitation of Two-Thirds World resources, the creation of a welfare state, emigration, and industrialization.

But the post-war phenomenon in Asian, African, and Latin American mega-cities is an apparently irresolvable conflict between over-urbanization, due to too rapid a migration of millions to the capital cities, and a slow industrialization providing too few jobs. Migrants swell the ranks of the under-employed and unemployed. New urbanites adjust to their environment by creating permanent slums, which are now far beyond the control of any planning or administrative body.

SOME CITIES IN ASIA
(POPULATION IN MILLIONS)[4]

	1980	2000	2010
Seoul	8.3	9.9	9.9
Kolkuta (Calcutta)	9.0	12.9	15.6
Mumbai (Bombay)	8.1	18.1	23.6
Metro-Manila	6.0	10.9	13.9
Jakarta	6.0	11.0	15.3
Delhi	5.6	11.7	15.1
Shanghai	11.7	12.9	13.7
Karachi	5.0	11.8	16.6
Beijing	9.0	10.8	11.5
Tianjin	7.3	9.2	10.0
Bangkok	4.7	7.3	9.0

The number of Asian cities with a population of more than one million will rise from 64 in 1980 to 133 in the year 2020, and their combined population will increase from 185,000,000 to 639,000,000.[5] In most of these mega-cities the slum population grows faster than the rest of the population, from rates of 30 percent up to 75 percent in some cities.

For example, when the slum population of Manila began growing during the sixties it made up a quarter of the population. Approximately 60 percent of Metro-Manila's population can be classified as low income, and more than 2.5 million people—many of them squatters—live in slums or depressed areas.[5] Peter Lloyd writes:

> The greatest rates of growth for squatters have occurred in national capitals. Industry, dominated by transnational companies, has preferred the capital city—often a seaport and close to the political leadership of the country, technical skills and services are more readily available, and the city elite providing a greater part of its local market. The government bureaucracies administering the expanding social services are largely located in the capitals. So instead of a hierarchy of urban centers evenly spaced along a continuum, we find the capital cities embracing an ever-increasing proportion of the national population, far outdistancing their nearest rivals.[6]

Metro-Manila, for example, is eight times the size of the second largest Filipino city, Davao.

Tatalon: a slum of hope

The physical characteristics and culture of each shantytown (slum, squatter community, *favela,* or *bustee*) differ from country to country. Yet the process that generates them and the resulting evils are universal among the major cities of Two-Thirds World countries.

We may consider two kinds of slums:

(a) Inner city slums

Inner cities have decaying tenements and houses in what were once good middle- and upper-class neighborhoods. Lloyd describes these areas as "slums of despair," where those who have lost the will to try and those who cannot cope gravitate. Here too are recent immigrants who have come to be near employment opportunities and students in the hundreds of thousands, seeking the upward mobility of education.

In such an atmosphere of despair and deterioration, social forces and expectations work against a responsiveness to the gospel. It appears more strategic to work in the second kind of slum—peripheral shantytowns—where social forces and expectations create a high degree of receptivity to the gospel.

(b) Peripheral shantytowns

Spontaneous communities built around massive cities tend to be "slums of hope," whose longer established occupants have employment and are now seeking to build their own homes. Yet here, too, are people and clusters of despair.

The shantytown of Tatalon in Manila is an example of one of the many slums that have sprung up since World War II. It lies halfway between Manila City and Quezon City, two cities that are part of Metro-Manila.

The story of Tatalon begins with the oppression of the Spanish. At one point the Spanish propagated a law regarding the need to file for titles to land. Since the peasants knew little Spanish, they were unaware of the law and unable to gain titles to their lands. Those families close to the Spaniards utilized the law for their own ends. Eventually, just a few families owned the land around Manila in vast tracts.

One of these families was that of J. M. Tuason. He owned the land now known as the Tatalon Estate. Dating back to the pre-war period, the Tatalon Estate's history was characterized by claims, counter-claims, controversies, and court cases between J. M. Tuason and Co. and several other claimants.

In the thick of ownership controversies that have taken place in the area over the past forty years, the steady growth of an unwanted population in Tatalon has been barely noticed. Despite a total absence of facilities and services, provincial migrants flooding into the Metro-Manila areas found the unoccupied land of Tatalon an ideal site for establishing a foothold in the big city.

Social unrest began gripping the area, almost reaching the boiling point in the late 1950's when Tuason and his administrator, Araneta, carried out mass eviction and demolition on the basis of an "authority to eject" issued by the courts.

I learned of the battles that raged when I sat one evening with Aling Cita, leader of the women. "In those days Araneta came in with bulldozers to bulldoze down the squatter homes," she recalled. "We put them up the next night. Sometimes we surrounded the bulldozers. Some people lay down in front of them so they could not move. It was during that time that the old man up on the hill had his face beaten, so his lip became twisted and curled and his teeth were broken. He was one of the first people here—our leader. He was beaten by Araneta's henchmen."

Today, the average home in Tatalon contains 12.3 people. There are 14,500 in this six-block community—a density of 57,500 people per square kilometer. Homes were first putup by the river. Because of regular flooding, many were then relocated on higher ground.

Tatalon is one of the more fortunate squatter areas. The government in the last few years has established a sites and services program, gradually upgrading the area. It has put in roads, a number of toilets and some water pumps, surveyed the land, and organized the people. Those longest in residence can buy the small lot on which they live at a reasonable cost.

This program has evolved from a responsiveness to people's needs over a number of years.

"Through all the turmoil the community came together," Aling Cita told me proudly. "As time went on, the National Housing Authority was able to buy the land from Araneta. Now the squatters can own their own land. I went to General Tobias

17

myself and asked him to put in the water pumps. These are better days."

Tatalon is a place of hope, a slum in which to dream and to aspire, a community that is beginning (with a lot of help) to come through decades of suffering into a little economic security. The people are gradually obtaining land and water. Enough individuals in the community have found employment to spur the others on. In such a context, the gospel is welcome as one more social change people are going through. It can move like a wildfire.

NOTES

1. *World Fact Book.* http://www.cia.gov/cia/publications/factbook/fields/ 2004.html. Accessed June 2004, Figures estimates for 2002.

2. *World Fact Book.* http://www.cia.gov/cia/publications/factbook/geos/ rp.html. Accessed June 2004

3. UN, *World Population Prospects* (1999), 96.

4. UNCHS (Habitat), *State of the World's Cities* (Nairobi:UNCHS, 2001), 11.

5. UNCHS (Habitat), *State of the World's Cities* (Nairobi:UNCHS, 2001), appendix.

6. Peter Lloyd, *Slums of Hope? Shanty Towns of the Third World* (Pelican Books, 1979), 21, 33. Reprinted by permission of Penguin Books Ltd.

Chapter Two

Never the Same Again

FACE TO FACE WITH POVERTY

The people of Tatalon had good reason to wonder why a white New Zealander would move into Aling Nena's home. Many of my friends were also wondering why I had left a ministry among Manila's middle class to live with the poor. However, the decision to move to the slum was not made on a whim. It was one step in a journey of carrying the cross. In this cross are meaning, reality, and destiny. Only in this cross are there ultimate answers to the deep questions that are the wellspring of human life and experience.

I first learned of the impact of that cross as a ten-year-old. While hunting for books in the uppermost garret of Dunedin, New Zealand's oak-paneled public library, I discovered a treasure trove of biographies of famous Christians. One was to set the direction of my life. It was the story of a sickly, bespectacled man—Toyohiko Kagawa of Japan.[1]

As a student, Kagawa realized that if the slum people of neighboring Shinkawa were to be saved, he must move there and preach the gospel. The poor would never accept something offered by the wealthy and respectable who came from across the river, dispensed their charitable gospel, and then returned home. A church planted in the slums must be tended day and night.

On Christmas Day 1909, Kagawa, twenty-one years old, frustrated after efforts to persuade his superiors of the needs of the poor, packed his belongings into a little handcart, crossed the bridge, and walked into the slums of Shinkawa to serve his

Lord. For the next fourteen years and eight months, he lived there, teaching, preaching the gospel, and ministering to the poor.

He became a strategic figure in the development of the labor unions of Japan, brought widespread reforms to stem the flow of the poor to the cities, was a key man in the reconstruction of Tokyo after it was devastated by the 1923 earthquake, helped fashion a law that abolished slums, and was a leader in the reconstruction of Japan after World War II.

In all these activities, he constantly proclaimed the cross. He inspired nationwide evangelistic campaigns, preached to the country's political leaders and to the Emperor himself, and established many churches and Bible schools among the poor. Thousands entered the kingdom through his life.

It was the truth I learned as a child, an unquestioned assumption learned from Kagawa—living among the poor is the only possible way to plant the Christian faith among them.

Kagawa chose the rugged, rough-hewn cross of his pauper Master. He chose the suffering of the cross. With the wisdom gained from a good education, he could have been rich. But the poverty he chose shows his true wisdom.

We, too, must reach the poor. The cross is our method, the cross is our message, and the cross is our life.

Kagawa once wrote:

> In the blood-drops dripping
> Along the sorrowful road to the Via Dolorosa
> Will be written the story of man's regeneration.
> Tracing the blood-stained and staggering footprints
> Let me go forward!
> This day also must my blood flow, following
> In that blood-stained pattern.[2]

Rugged cross or jeweled replica?

After training and preparation, I was sent from New Zealand to Manila as a missionary. During my first year in Manila, I lived with a missionary and his family, serving and learning from him, and assisting in his ministry of teaching discipleship in a Bible school. I taught two classes of 60 students.

I recruited nine of these students to join me, under the leadership of an experienced missionary, in establishing a predominantly middle-class church.[3]

Theologians and church-growth specialists would say that we were on the forefront of missions, the cutting edge of the great commission, the thick of the battle to establish new beachheads for the gospel.

But my life was unfulfilled. The philosopher within me found no answers to the search for meaning; the artist found no fulfillment in the search for perfection and ultimate truth; the leader had not found the center of destiny and purpose towards which to lead others. All three voices told me I still was far from the place of God's call.

I became relatively proficient at passing on skills and programs, reproducing laborers who could pass on skills and programs to other believers. But was this the discipleship of Jesus? My students came from poor families. For many, Bible college became the stepping-stone to economic security as a paid "professional" pastor. My own wealth, and our deliberate focus on a middle-class target group, precluded me from passing on the disciplines of the Beatitudes: poverty of spirit, meekness, peacemaking (bringing justice with love)—qualities at the heart of discipleship.

The cross I was carrying and handing on was only a half-size one. I realized my life must portray a dramatically different picture of ministry if I wanted to lead these men and women into the way of the cross. Discipleship had to be taught in the context of a Jesus-style ministry to the poor—in the context of rejecting pride and status seeking, power, and economic security.

A thief in the slums

Cross-centered discipleship came into sharp focus the week I visited the home of one of my students. He lived in the slums of a pineapple factory in Mindanao, the large southern island of the Philippines.

We traveled by jeepney. Four people sat in the front seat, seven sat along the sides, and another four hung precariously along the back in various ways—all laughing and talking in unknown dialects. A load of vegetables sat on my feet, and chickens squawked under the seat.

We stopped at a military outpost. A soldier cautiously inspected each passenger, and then climbed aboard the front seat to provide protection from rebels, bandits, or guerillas. Villagers stared at us from small nipa huts huddled along the road.

Finally, we arrived at Lario's home on a pineapple plantation, stretching for mile after mile on land confiscated or bought from hundreds of peasant farmers.

For the first time, I saw the effects of Western consumerism in the Two-Thirds World. Accumulated profits are taken to America, juggled between three different companies. Meanwhile, 7000 workers, many of them former owners of the land on which they now work, live on a pitiful wage in one square mile of squatter homes. The transnational company argues that at least these workers have some income. But they deliberately keep this below subsistence level in order to circumvent union troubles. We Westerners eat the canned pineapple produced, with little thought for the social and economic process behind it.

Lario's house consisted of bamboo posts and pieces of wood he had scrounged from the dump and elsewhere. As I stooped through the door, the first thing I did was put my foot through the floorboards.

They called in all their *utang* (the debts of old friends) to feed me, and gave me their blanket, a mosquito net, and a sleeping mat.

Lario's mother and father both work. During my visit, his father was ill with a skin disease on his legs. Their income could not provide enough money for medicine.

The toilet had blown over in a typhoon, so Lario and I began to dig a deep hole. The neighbors came to see this Americano. They had never seen a white person work with his hands before.

"Hey. Joe, what are you doing?" I had learned that Filipinos call white men "Joe" because of the many American soldiers who had lived there over the last century.

"I'm digging a toilet," I answered. "Why don't you come over this evening? We will preach the gospel and explain why!"

In the afternoon, I talked with Lario's mother. As she ironed with a charcoal iron, she told the story of their poverty, of the personal tragedy that had caused it and the oppression that had perpetuated it. Tears fell. She told of how the Lord had sustained her, how in him alone was her comfort.

As evening came, smoke from the wood fire wafted through the house, driving away the mosquitoes. Estella, Lario's twelve-year-old sister, picked up a homemade wooden guitar and began to sing of the Lord who understands the pain and sorrow of his children, who is building a mansion "just over the hilltop."

"*Mahirap*," she said to me sadly at the end of her song. "Life is so hard, so poor."

In the light of the kerosene lamp, we ate our rice and fish for supper. Then we placed a lantern outside and set up some bamboo for seats. It was Easter Friday, and I began to speak about the cross.

The lantern cast its eerie light on the tattered clothes of the men sitting on the bamboo seats we had made. It was quiet. One could sense the listening ears of neighbors in the surrounding houses as they sat in their windows. They listened to the story of those nails that shattered his wrists, the jolting of that wooden post as they dropped it into the ground, the blood flowing from his crown of thorns.

I spoke of the thief beside Jesus who cried, "Jesus, remember me," and of Jesus' reply, "This day you will be with me in paradise." Samson, a big denim-clad youth sitting at the front, began to weep quietly. He, too, had been a thief. He repented, and the Spirit of God entered his life.

In the midst of this twentieth-century scene—surrounded by the poor, in the presence of the Spirit of God, declaring the cross—I was aware that I was standing in the central stream of history. Two thousand years earlier, with a similar pair of dusty sandals on his feet, my Lord had declared his destiny with these words: "The Spirit of the Lord is upon me because he has anointed me to preach the gospel to the poor" (Luke 4:18).

Here also the pauper apostles of history had stood through the centuries. Here was meaning, destiny, and truth, enough to satisfy the deepest searchings of the human heart.

The proclamation of the cross stands at the center of all meaning. In it justice and truth, mercy and compassion meet. But it is framed by suffering, poverty, and the pain of humanity. It is framed by the poor.

The dignity, the human quality of the leadership of Jesus, had captivated me as a child and brought me into his kingdom. Like the disciples who had walked before me throughout history, God had overwhelmed me with his love.

But once we know him, we continue to seek him. "I count everything as loss because of the surpassing worth of knowing Christ Jesus my Lord" (Philippians 3:8).

Where can Jesus be found and known today? To find him, we must go where he is. Did he not say, "Where I am, there shall my servant be also"?

Such a search invariably leads us into the heart of poverty. For Jesus always goes to the point of deepest need. Where there is suffering, he will be there binding wounds. His compassion eternally drives him to human need. Where there is injustice, he is there. His justice demands it. He does not dwell on the edge of the issues. He is involved, always doing battle with the fiercest of the forces of evil and powers of darkness.

That night, in a squatter settlement on a pineapple plantation, my heart found rest. There could be no turning back from God's call. I must preach the gospel to the poor.

In a heap of ruins

After the week with Lario and his family, I returned to Manila, asking myself, *Where would Jesus be involved if he were in Manila?*

One day I climbed to the top of a one-hundred-foot-high mountainous pile of rotting, decaying food and rubbish. I looked at the shacks of 10,000 of Manila's poorest and at their emaciated figures scavenging paper, bottles, and cans to resell them to middlemen who would then recycle them.

The people had work—they were happy in that. I watched as little children, older women, and comparatively healthy workers picked their way through the pile. They carried their goods in sacks on their shoulders back to their homes, where the goods were sorted and classified.

I walked through the squatter community. The smell was indescribable. Sickness was rife. The houses were constructed from old sacks, metal, and other old garbage. Children reached out their hands in laughter to touch me, but pulled back when they saw my tears. As I wept, my heart cried out in anger. *Lord, how long can you permit the degradation and destruction of your people? Why don't you do something?*

Suddenly, I knew his answer: "I have done something. Two thousand years ago I stepped into poverty in the person of my Son. And I have dwelt there ever since in the person of my sons and daughters. Today I am calling for other sons and daughters to enter into the poverty of the poor in order to bring my kingdom to them."

Jesus would dwell today wherever there is need. Here, in the slums of Manila, the Prince would become one of the paupers: "For you know the grace of our Lord Jesus Christ, that though he was rich, yet for your sake he became poor that by his poverty you might become rich" (2 Corinthians 8:9).

Here, among the poorest of the poor, he would preach, heal, and bring justice.

Job described these poor: "Yet does not one in a heap of ruins stretch out his hand, and in his disaster, cry for help? Did not I weep for him whose day was hard? Was not my soul grieved for the poor?" (Job 30:24–25).

It would be in a "heap of ruins" such as this smoldering rubbish heap, a modern-day urban Gehenna, that Jesus himself would minister.

Four hundred communities

In 1978 the National Housing Authority of the Philippines identified 415 squatter communities in Metro-Manila. Of these, they identified 253 as communities that could be upgraded on site. In the remaining 162 communities, the demolition and relocation of unwanted squatter settlements by truckloads of armed men would proceed.

Yet Jesus would have ministered to these very people. Surely we too must live among them, bringing them the tangible blessing of his kingdom. His compassion compels. The cross compels. The search for meaning and reality compels.

We must call men to that task and place the cross where the battle is hardest fought. The church must not only be planted; it must be planted where the gospel has never been known. And where but among the poor of these cities is a harder place to plant the church?

Our ideals, however, are constantly limited by the realities of our humanity and its incipient sinfulness, both personal and collective. Identification with or among the poor cannot be accomplished in a day, a week, or even a month. A missionary must always limit his own idealism.

I needed to move in this new direction harmoniously with the body of co-workers in which God had placed me. I needed to build a ministry to the poor on the solid foundation of Scripture. My idea of disciplemaking had to be refined. The attainment of my calling to Manila's poor would take time.

NOTES

1. Comments on Kagawa are taken from Cyril J. Davey, *Kagawa of Japan* (Epworth Press, 1960).
2. Toyohiko Kagawa. "The Cross of the Whole Christ," in *Meditations on the Cross* (SCM, 1936), 16.
3. For a study of this church-planting venture see Cary Perdue, "The Case of the Kamu Bible Christian Fellowship," *Asia Pulse* (Evangelical Missions Information Service, Box 794, Wheaton, Illinois 60187, July 1982), Vol. 15, No. 3.

Chapter Three

God's Happy Poor
THE POOR IN THE SCRIPTURES

Questions continually rolled around my mind: "Why are the poor, poor?" "Why are they blessed?" "Which poor are blessed?" "Why does James call them rich in faith?" "Who are the poor Jesus spoke of?"

To understand what Jesus wanted us to do for the poor, I sat down with a friend one day and copied out every verse in the Bible about the poor onto small, white cards. I carried them with me for four years. They were my meditation day and night. They determined every major decision.

My concordance to the Bible listed 245 references to "the poor," "poverty," or "lack" in the Old Testament of the English Scriptures. They made an interesting study. There were five main root words:[1]

> *Ebyon*: needy and dependent (61 times)
>
> *Dal*: the frail poor, the weak (57 times)
>
> *Rush*: the impoverished through dispossession (31 times)
>
> *Chaser*: to suffer lack of bread and water, to hunger (36 times)
>
> *Ani*: poverty caused by affliction and oppression (80 times)

In the New Testament the word Jesus uses for "poor," *ptochos,* is the translation of the word *anaw,* which in turn is derived from *ani.*[2] *Anaw* at times means "the humble," but elsewhere, as in

Isaiah 61:1 from which Jesus quotes, it has the meaning of "the oppressed poor."

The concept of poverty and the analysis of its causes and effects change as the history of God's dealing with his people progresses. Before the monarchy of David and Solomon, in the Pentateuch, and in Job, societies were built essentially around extended family or clan structures. Riches were the blessing of God; poverty was brought about by some misfortune or through judgment of personal sin. The poor man was to be helped from his poverty.

From the time of the monarchy, a center of privileged people began to develop. Excavations in Tirzeh indicate that before the monarchy all houses had similar dimensions and furnishings. During the 8th century B.C. however, different districts had come into being: a well-to-do neighborhood for the rich; slums for the poor.

The rich began to treat the poor as though they belonged to a lower order. Poverty came to be seen as a much deeper deficiency in a person, particularly in the Wisdom literature (the Book of Proverbs and so on).

The poor, for their part, began to see their poverty as synonymous with being oppressed. The standard expression, "who oppresses the poor," attributes the cause of poverty to the rich.

Hence, we find the prophets denouncing constantly the rich (called the oppressor or the unrighteous) and upholding the "godly poor."

These are the ani, the oppressed poor with whom Jesus identified—"the poor of Yahweh." "Poor in spirit" is an expression primarily describing this social class and its response to such oppression.

God's plan for ministry

Suddenly, in the midst of these new revelations about the poor, my plans seemed to crumble in front of my eyes. After years of work, building relationships, molding ideas, and building together, the leadership of the mission I worked under went through a time of turmoil, related to this need to "preach the gospel to the poor." I returned to New Zealand.

But God was faithful. The relationships I had built with Filipino Christians opened the door back into Manila *and* to a ministry with the poor. Because of their commitment to the poor, some of my Filipino friends had established an indigenous discipling movement called REACH. I began my work in Manila again, this time under their auspices, determined to avoid being trapped into a middle-class missionary lifestyle. This time, I wanted to dwell among the poor. I wanted to enter into the knowledge of God. I wanted to learn to die to self, to security, to my own culture, to my wealth.

The first step was to learn the language and culture of the poor. I boarded a crowded bus for a small city in a Tagalog province. Here I was to study the language of Manila's poor, Tagalog, in one of its purest provincial forms.

I prayed: *Lord, I have no home here, no contacts, but I'm sure you'll provide. Find me the poorest families. Since I'm unused to living among the poor, let it be a well-built home, with a good toilet so I can maintain my health.*

The historic Catholic cathedral in the town of 100,000 was full of images of saints, and there was only one Protestant church. I walked to the pastor's house and asked for accommodation for a few days. Although he was gracious, I could see that he could ill afford to provide for me. I had known this man when he had been a fine preacher in a city church. He had chosen to minister to the rural poor at no little cost.

After two days with the pastor, the pastor's assistant came to take me to his home. We traveled by tricycle (a motorbike with a highly decorated and stylized sidecar costing about five cents a ride) along the half-formed muddy tracks into the unfinished government subdivision. The local wisdom was that corrupt government officials had embezzled the development funds through various means. As we rode along the track, I drew shy smiles and calls of "Hey, Joe!"

When we arrived at the house, I thanked the Lord. It was perfect.

Ka Emilio, the father (sixty-eight years of age), told how the family had constructed the house in one week at a cost of $130. It was all I'd prayed for: concrete walls and a tin roof (or a "G.I. sheet" as Filipinos call it). The toilet had a concrete floor, with enough room to "shower" by scooping water with a tin can from a plastic bucket. An old frog and some neighborly lizards shared it with us. Next to my bedroom was the community pump.

We put in a bunk above my friend's bed. We had to push the wall out six inches since I was ill suited to a Filipino-sized bed. This gave us a five-by-six foot bedroom to share.

Ka Emilio was a man of old Tagalog dignity, a gracious and hospitable host. He coughed constantly, with one lung rotted by tuberculosis. He maintained his health by planting and watering vegetables and the trees around his home.

I knew no Tagalog and he knew no English, but we had many long conversations. Once he described the Japanese invasion of their city, complete with dive-bombing and its effects on the frightened people, all in dramatized Tagalog.

He taught me much of the dignity and pride of the Tagalog people whom I had come to serve. While living in Ka Emilio's house, I saw the biblical concepts of poverty take flesh in the community around me.

The poor who lack

I ate next door at his daughter and son-in-law's home, but I would watch Ka Emilio cooking his rice. At times all he had to eat with his rice were the leaves off the trees he'd planted.

Job 30:3–4 tells us of such poor: "Through want and hard hunger they gnaw the dry and desolate ground; they pick mallow and the leaves of bushes and to warm themselves the roots of broom."

Ka Emilio was one of the chaser: those who lack the basic necessities of life, those who want.

At nights I would lie sweating on my plywood bed and search for answers. *Why was he poor? How could such a poor man be blessed?* A study of the word chaser told me some causes of this kind of poverty.

Proverbs tells us that wickedness causes the belly to suffer want (13:25); too much sleep and want will attack us like an armed robber (6:10–11); hasty planning leads to want (21:5); oppressing the poor to increase our own wealth or giving to the rich (22:16), loving pleasure (21:17), or miserliness and gambling (28:22) all bring us to want. This poverty is caused by personal sins.

The Scriptures also speak of the solution: "The Lord is my shepherd, I shall not want" (Psalm 23:1). "Those who seek the Lord lack no good thing" (Psalm 34:10).

One day through an evangelistic crusade, Ka Emilio came to believe that Christ had died for him. I gave him a Tagalog Bible in comic form (the poor read comics, not books). Perhaps time would lead him to a complete obedience to this Lord who is Shepherd, and this would lead him and his family out of want.

Even then, I knew that such a solution was insufficient. Deeper causes to poverty than personal problems—communal and national and global problems—require biblical solutions at each appropriate level.

But I needed to begin at the level of the personal and spiritual and explore outward. We tried raising rabbits to supplement Ka Emilio's income. When that failed. I bought him a goat, but he eventually sold it as he was too old to constantly take it out to feed. Ultimately, the solution to Ka Emilio's poverty was a son who got a job in Saudi Arabia and sent back American dollars.

Poverty and sin

Some poverty is caused by sin. But poverty also causes sin. The broken social structure of the squatter areas creates an environment which exercises little social control over sin. Poverty causes people to steal.

Proverbs 30:8–9 offers this sound advice: "Give me neither poverty nor riches: feed me with the food that is needful for me, lest I be full, and deny thee, and say, 'Who is the Lord?' or lest I be poor, and steal, and profane the name of my God."

A favorite meal in the Philippines is cooked dog meat and beer. One day I was walking round the corner of the track and came across three men quietly pushing a jeepney loaded with dogs. They had stolen them and would sell them to a restaurant for meat. That same week I passed a truck. People were draining it of gasoline.

Ninety percent proof

Poverty also causes drunkenness. The first thing one notices among areas of poverty is drunken men. Everywhere there are groups of men drinking—at all times from morning to night. Drunkenness and alcoholism cause destitution, but most drunkenness among the squatters is a result of the poverty in which the men find themselves.

Unemployment results in drunkenness. Even Proverbs indicates this. When it advises against kings becoming drunk, it suggests: "Give strong drink to him who is perishing, and wine to those in bitter distress; let them drink and forget their poverty, and remember their misery no more" (Proverbs 31:6–7). (We should not interpret this as a license for the poor to drink, but rather as a plea for sober kings!)

One Filipino study of a slum community indicated that 68 percent of the employable adults are unemployed.[3] In Tatalon it was 42 percent.[4] Drinking with friends is a way to fill up the day and drown out the sorrow, despair, and lack of self–respect inherent in unemployment.

Ka Emilio's two sons became my good companions. Living with them, I began to understand why they were poor and why they were often drunk. Seraphim had been a soldier but lost his job and income for two years because of an injury. In my diary one night I jotted:

> Tonight Seraphim will drink himself to sleep. It is hard to be without work. If he had work, he could get married. His girlfriend is already working and has graduated. He melancholically plays his guitar on the doorstep as the sun sets. A man of dignity, a soldier of honor seeking to maintain his dignity with the Beatles and a bottle. How do I help his soul and body? How can this poor man be blessed except in the kingdom?

What is the solution to drunkenness? Some years before I had traveled through a valley in Bukidnon. The homes were among the poorest I had seen—thatched huts, only a few meters square. I asked around to discover why. A local rice wine was ninety percent proof. Everybody drank it. Thirteen or fourteen year-old pregnant girls drank it. Children were born to drunken mothers and so grew up with the taste and desire for wine. People died before they were thirty. So it went on for generation after generation.

Then an older lady missionary came in and started an orphanage. From this base, the good news spread. The preaching of the gospel broke that cycle. *Chaser,* those whose personal sins have caused poverty, are blessed by receiving God's kingdom.

The poverty of immorality

Poverty provides an environment not only for drunkenness, but also for immorality. In the immediate cluster of houses around our home, very few couples were legally married. Many of the women had lived with two or three husbands. A number of men had a *kabit* (a second wife). In one survey we did informally, over 30 percent of the men indicated that they had become squatters as a result of some form of immorality—often in the process of "eloping" or taking a new wife and hence leaving their provincial home.

Squatter areas seem to be the ultimate collecting pot for the moral outcasts of society. Perhaps this is because they are areas where social norms and values have broken down almost totally, with immorality and infidelity running unchecked and unashamed.

In a survey of the forty-three neediest families in one slum area, only one-sixth of those interviewed had been legally married when first living with their wife.[5] Six men and four women had been previously married. The figures are symbols of pain, anguish and frustration.

Types of initial union	Families	% of sample
Church marriage	2	4.65
Civil marriage	5	11.63
Living together	4	9.30
Elopement and living together	17	39.54
Cheated and living together	7	16.28
Raped and living together	7	16.28
Polygamous household	1	2.32
Total	43	100.00

Frustration over broken relationships erupted one day when I was sitting in my upstairs room, preparing a message in Tagalog.

Suddenly, I heard an angry voice in the rooms below: "I'm going to leave him! I'll file a law suit!"

Two or three neighboring relatives rapidly materialized to quiet down their niece, each passing on a piece of advice.

"The best thing is to stay with him," one lady said. "I remember when I first heard that the *Bombay* (Manilan terminology for an Indian—her late husband had been one) had another woman. I was furious. So I followed his jeepney and watched. They met at a bookstand, so I went and talked nicely to her. I didn't let her know I was his wife. She told me she had three children also. I have even had her children in my home when she could not cope!"

Her daughter added her own story: "I cried for months when the father of my son married her, but I've learned to forgive."

But the woman in distress would not be quieted. What could she do? He had another woman! There were many discussions during the next few days as the women sat for hours at a time, analyzing what options were open when their common-law husbands moved on to the next woman. Would they remain faithful themselves? Should they find another, take revenge, or move out of the community?

Immorality creates poverty by generating bitterness, jealousy, insecurity, family disorganization, hatred, and murder. It is difficult for a man adequately to support more than one family. When relationships have been destroyed and broken, it is difficult for the children to learn how to relate to any form of authority, or develop the management skills necessary for many jobs.

Personal sins help create poverty. Poverty, in turn, provides an environment for personal sin. This kind of poverty is only transformed by a gospel and a discipleship that enables people to be freed from these sins.

The dependent poor

Of course, not all poverty is related to personal sin. The words ebyon and dal describe another kind of poor. Ebyon is the designation of the person who finds himself begging: the needy, the dependent.

Job indicates the appropriate response to these ebyon when he describes his personal identification with those in need: "I was eyes to the blind and feet to the lame. I was father to the poor, (ebyon) and I searched out the cause of him whom I did not know" (Job 29:15–16).

Job's response was the only possible response we could give when we met a deaf and dumb stowaway. We had parked a borrowed jeep downtown after transporting some people back to Manila from a conference. It was late, but the crowds continued hustling and bustling. A boy in ragged clothes indicated he would watch our jeep for us and make sure that no one stole it. We nodded agreement, knowing that for many boys this was their only income.

On returning, we gave him a *peso* for his trouble. He signaled his thanks, but seemed strangely silent. He went and sat down again in the shop doorway.

I got into the driver's seat, but the compassion of Christ would not let me start the jeep.

"Do you think he's deaf?" I asked my companion, a social worker.

She nodded. I sat and thought. How could I return home to my luxury and leave one in such destitution?

"Let's go talk with him," I said suddenly, leaping out of the jeep and squatting beside him. I tried speaking, but he just nodded his head. Fortunately, my companion had some training in sign language.

"I came from Cebu (a city on an island south of Manila)," the boy signed to us. "I stowed away on a boat. It traveled three days and three nights. I arrived in Manila with three *pesos* in my pocket."

The signs were accompanied with fear and hope. My friend translated them into English.

"Why did you leave home?" I asked.

"Why did you leave home?" she signed.

He nodded and with great rapidity of hand action explained. "They always used to laugh at me. My father used to beat me because I was deaf."

She translated. I nodded.

"Where do you live?" she signed.

His home was a six-by-three-foot packing case, slotted among the others by the river.

I knew about a restaurant in the park that was staffed by people from a school for the deaf. We signed to him that we would meet him the next day and take him there. Eventually, he began attending a school for the deaf run by some fine Catholic laymen. Some years later, I heard that he was successfully working as a chicken farmer.

This type of poverty is not caused by sin; it is poverty caused by natural calamity. When John the Baptist queried Jesus, "Are you he who is to come, or shall we look for another?" Jesus spoke of these poor in his response: "The blind receive their sight and the lame walk, lepers are cleansed, and the deaf hear" (Matthew 11:3–5).

Jesus also describes them quoting Deuteronomy 15:11: "For the poor (ebyon) will never cease out of the land, therefore I command you, 'You shall open wide your hand to your brother, to the needy (ebyon) and to the poor (ani) in the land.'"

It is to these ebyon that God's kingdom brings healing and socio-economic uplift.

Too frail to work

"Oy, Kumusta?" (How are you?) I asked. "How's your job-hunting going?"

She smiled sadly and answered. "I can't take a job."

"Oh, why is that?" She had studied in the same class as Coring, who was typing for me at the plywood table of my kitchen-cum-office.

"I'm too weak. I cannot work five days a week, so I cannot take a job." She looked away from my eyes, staring at the drawn-back sack that acted as a curtain.

I felt something of the sorrow God must feel for such people. Who would rescue these poor? Poverty is frailty and weakness. In Hebrew the root word is *dal.* This word is connected with the word *dallah,* the "class of the poor."

The Old Testament (2 Kings 24:14) describes the poorest in the land who were left behind during the exile to Babylon.

Jeremiah (5:4) tells us that these poor ones were looked down upon, while Job (20:19) tells us that they are easily crushed and abandoned, without the means to recover from loss or calamity.

These dal are blessed in the kingdom. In the song of Hannah we read: "He raises up the poor (dal) from the dust; He lifts the needy (ebyon) from the ash heap, to make them sit with princes and inherit a seat of honor" (1 Samuel 2:8).

Husband of widows

Widows also fall into this category of those made poor by calamity.

Quietness stole softly over the slum, replacing the cacophony of the sound of a thousand people crowded into their plywood homes. The moon and the stars silhouetted the patchwork of old tires holding down the roofs from typhoons. It was midnight, the hour for quiet prayer.

My heart ached for the situation of the widow next door. She had been kind to me. My thoughts and eyes sought out the houses of other poor widows. I thought of the rice they'd cooked that night for their children, some without fish, meat, or vegetables.

Suddenly, I realized, *Lord, if you are the father of orphans, surely that makes you the husband of widows! They are especially yours!*

I began to pray for ways to help these women. They were poor through no sin of their own, nor even the sin of others. Their circumstances had simply happened. And so God takes responsibility for them: "The Lord watches over the sojourners. He upholds the widow and the fatherless" (Psalm 146:9). We, too, are to incarnate his love amongst these dallah.

Children of sweat

Children, too, are important to Jesus. They also belong among the frail and the weak—the dallah. How can one help but love children? As I walked down the back paths into the community, I would hear cries of *"Kuya Viv! Kuya Viv!"* ("Big brother Viv!"). Small children would laughingly greet me all the way until I reached my own house. Often we would play games together.

There is a Tagalog phrase, *"anak-pawis,"* which means "child of sweat" or "child of poverty." Ninety-two percent of children in the slums and 87 percent of the total population in the Philippines suffer from intestinal parasites. Sixty-nine percent of Filipino children under six years of age are in various stages of protein calorie malnutrition. A further 45 percent of them have first-degree malnutrition, meaning they are 10–24 percent below their standard weight.

Indelibly etched in my memory is a friend, holding in her arms a little child with swollen stomach, spindly arms, and a swollen head. He was sick and retching constantly. She tried to comfort him while telling me that when his father came home, she would get some money for medicine. I knew he had no money to bring her. On the mat slept five of her other eleven children.

John the Apostle said: "If anyone has the world's goods and sees his brother in need, yet closes his heart against him, how does God's love abide in him?" (1 John 3:17).

Poverty is dispossession

There is yet another cause of poverty beyond the realm of personal sin and the calamities of life. This is poverty caused by the sins of the rich, the leaders of a people, or the oppression of a conquering nation. Two Hebrew words are related to this: rush and ani.

Rush refers to the dispossessed poor, the impoverished. Such is the poverty of the tenant farmers forced off their lands to make way for the multinational sugar and banana plantations or because of unfair land reform.

Proverbs 13:23 tells us: "The fallow ground of the poor yields much food, but it is swept away through injustice." Many squatters come to Manila because their livelihoods have been swept away by injustice. This is essentially a passive phenomenon. It is the people being disinherited—first in the province, then in the city.

God looks for an intercessor who will seek justice for these poor: "But this is a people robbed and plundered; . . . they have become a prey with none to rescue, a spoil with none to say 'Restore!'" (Isaiah 42:22).

White slavery

The dispossessed also include slaves. Aling Ada's daughter was taken by a syndicate that enslaves girls in drugs and prostitution. These syndicates of "white slavery," as it is called, jail girls in barred houses and force them into prostitution. After a few years, the girls are not only physically but also emotionally enslaved for life. Miraculously, Aling Ada's daughter escaped a week after she was abducted.

People refer to darkest Africa or General William Booth's "In Darkest England." The tourist belts in the Asian cities can rightly be called darkest Asia.

As slum statistics are unmentioned in the formal record books of Asian nations, so slavery is officially not spoken of. In the provinces, recruiters tempt girls with offers of good jobs in Manila. But upon reaching the city, they find themselves locked into these "safe houses" from which there is no escape. Once forced into the trade, the desire and ability to escape such a lifestyle goes. Few get out.[6]

Others are sold by employment agencies to men in the Middle East, Italy, Japan, Hong Kong, and elsewhere, often under the guise of being waitresses or house girls.

Bangkok's population, for example, of 8.3 million includes a small army of 60,000 women, mostly prostitutes, working out of 350 go-go bars, 130 massage parlors, and 100 dance halls.

Women who make the sex business successful in Bangkok see few profits for themselves. Travel agents skim off 50 percent of the take, bars and brothels pocket most of the remainder, leaving varying cuts from that share for the girls.

"We are down to our last resource," says Karinina David, a professor of community development at the University of the Philippines. "Once you sell your women and debase your culture, there is not much left."

Amos pronounces God's judgment on a nation for the same sin: "Because they sell the righteous for silver, and the needy for a pair of shoes—they that trample the head of the poor into the dust of the earth, and turn aside the way of the afflicted" (Amos 2:6–7).

God looks for women of commitment who will give their lives to rescue these girls. Women who accept this ministry must try to effect changes in the law to break the horrendous sale of flesh that parades itself under the name of tourism. It is a dangerous task. Two friends who tried to combat it at a government level were threatened so often they gave up. Yet Proverbs 31:9 says to continue to "open your mouth, judge righteously, maintain the rights of the poor and needy."

God looks for women who know that he will be their protector, as he was for Amy Carmichael and her band of women when they rescued temple prostitutes in India.

Who are the blessed poor?

The fifth Hebrew word used in the Old Testament is *ani* and its derivative *anaw* which is the word Jesus used when he talks of the blessed poor.

The root word means to bring low, to afflict, to ravish, to violate or force. It is used for a whole range of exercises in domination, such as when the people of Israel were afflicted by their taskmasters in Egypt (Exodus 1:11). It was used also to denote the response of humble dependence on God to such oppression (Job 34:28; Psalms 34:6). The ani is one bowed down under pressure, one occupying a lowly position, one who finds himself in a dependent relationship. It means "the humble poor of Yahweh" or "God's poor ones."

People who are ani are not contrasted with the rich, but with people of violence, oppressors who turn aside the needy from justice and who rob the poor of their rights by making unjust laws and publishing burdensome decrees (Isaiah 10:1–2).

Much of the poverty of Two-Thirds World countries can be attributed to such causes. Several centuries of iniquitous decrees by both the Spanish and the rich 400 families that rule the Philippines have resulted in a society oppressed, afflicted, and impoverished.

These blessed poor, then, include the needy (ebyon), the frail (dal), the dispossessed (rush), and those who lack (chaser). But within these categories, underlying them is poverty caused by the ruthlessness of the powerful, who deny the rights of the poor and do not respond to their calamities.

Is poverty blessed?

God rebels against poverty, for it destroys his whole creation. Nowhere in the Bible is poverty an ideal, as it became with later mystics. Nowhere is poverty glorified or romanticized. The fact that the poor are sometimes, and with increasing frequency in the Scriptures, called righteous is not so much to their own credit. They are righteous because their oppressors are so terribly unrighteous. The poor are therefore righteous *in comparison with* the oppressor who withholds their rights.

Nor are the poor blessed because of their material lack or their economic class. This would ignore salvation by grace and imply that salvation is given according to economic and sociological status. Poverty is not blessed, but the poor are—those poor who become *disciples*. The Beatitudes were spoken to Christ's disciples. They were truly "the poor of Yahweh." Because of their poverty, they trusted in God in a spirit of dependence. Matthew 5:3 ("Blessed are the poor in spirit") and Luke 6:20 ("Blessed are you poor") are both expressions of this idea.

The solution: discipleship

In summary, we may split the causes of poverty into three main categories: poverty caused by personal sin (chaser); poverty caused by calamity (ebyon and dal); and poverty caused by oppression (ani, anaw and rush).

Discipleship changes the poverty caused by personal sin. Membership in God's kingdom brings love, releases guilt, heals bitterness, and breaks the power of drunkenness, immorality, and gambling. It results in a new motivation for work. Our response to such poverty must be to live among the poor and preach the gospel by deed and by word (see Chapter 9).

Discipleship changes the poverty of the frail and the weak, for true disciples will aid the widows and orphans, welcome the stranger and the refugee, and help the destitute. God's power can heal the blind and the deaf. Our response to such poverty is relief, economic projects, and protection of the weak (see chapter 10).

Discipleship also changes poverty caused by oppression, injustice, and exploitation. Disciples defend the oppressed poor by bringing justice (see chapter 11).

In the context of poverty, the gospel is a gospel both of judgment and of mercy. To the rich and oppressor it is a message of judgment and woe, requiring repentance. As Jesus says: "Woe to you that are rich, for you have received your consolation. Woe to you that are full now, for you shall hunger. Woe to you that laugh now, for you shall mourn and weep" (Luke 6:24–25).

But to the poor the gospel is a message of hope, if they would but repent and believe: "Come to me, all who labor and are heavy laden, and I will give you rest"(Matthew 11:28).

To the poor, the gospel is a message of blessing, both now and in the future:

> Blessed are you poor, for yours is the kingdom of God. Blessed are you that hunger now, for you shall be satisfied. Blessed are you that weep now, for you shall laugh (Luke 6:20–21).

The poor receive the kingdom gladly now. But there will come a day when all oppression will cease and the unjust receive their dues. On that day, the poor will laugh and leap for joy, for each will have his mansion. There will be no more pain, no more sorrow, no more tears!

Blessed are you poor, for yours is—and shall be—the kingdom of God!

NOTES

1. For a fuller analysis, see Harvey L. Perkins. *The Poor and Oppressed: The Focus of Christian Participation in Human. Development,* Colleagues in Development: Bible Study Series, Singapore, Christian Conference of Asia (mimeo-series, 1977 to present). Also, Julio de Sta Ana, *Good News to the Poor* (Geneva: World Council of Churches, 1977).

2. Conrad Boerma, *"Rich Man, Poor Man—and The Bible"* (SCM, London 1979). Chapters 2 and 3 have a brief summary of the themes in the Bible related to poverty including a brief contrast between *ptochos,* the beggar, and *penes,* the industrious poor man.

3. F. Landa Jocano, *Slum as a Way of Life* (Quezon City: University of the Philippines Press, 1975), 31.

4. Figure from a description of the Tatalon Estate Zonal Improvement Project, furnished by the National Housing Authority, Quezon City.

5. Donald Denise Decaesstecker, *Impoverished Urban Filipino Families* (Manila: UST Press, 1978), 126. An in-depth study of the structure and problems of impoverished slum families in one of Manila's slums.

6. F. Landa Jocano, *op cit.,* chapter IX, "Deviant Females."

Chapter Four

Living as a Poor Man
LEARNING TO IDENTIFY

Two thousand years ago a seed fell from the sower's hand from heaven to earth. The God of eternity now inhabited humanity in the cry of a child, in the frame of a manger, in the tramp of sandaled feet.

But the symphony the angels sang at Jesus' birth was tinged by the melancholy of poverty. In coming from heaven to earth, the seed did not remain at the surface among the unrealities of the rich and the haughty. He buried himself in the depths of humanity. And those depths have weighed down the laboring poor for thousands of years.

The prophet Isaiah declared that God has two homes: "For thus says the high and lofty One who inhabits eternity, whose name is holy: I dwell in the high and holy place, and also with him who is of a contrite and humble-spirit" (Isaiah 57:15).

Two homes, two addresses: eternity and poverty.

The language of the poor

Real training in the knowledge of the God who dwells among the poor began by the flicker of a kerosene lamp, long before entering Tatalon, as I studied Tagalog in Ka Emilio's home. I began to learn the heartbeat, the soul, and the language of the poor.

After a long study session, I stood up for a stretch and went to the door. I looked out across the *nipa* thatch to the sky. The scene had all the drama of a traditional missionary movie scene, but beneath the romanticism lay the same melancholy of suffering Jesus knew.

Luz, Ka Emilio's daughter, and her husband Emy ran out of food each twentieth of the month. Over a period of time, we worked out a system where I paid the equivalent of the cost of my food in exchange for Ate Luz's cooking. Initially, in the style of Filipino hospitality, they gave me too much food until I explained that I should live on what they live on—though I asked them to add some extra meat to maintain my Vitamin B level. They improved their own food with the money earned by Ate Luz.

Learning the language of the poor

It is in the language of these poor that Jesus spoke. His Beatitudes, his Sermon on the Mount, made no sense to the rich of his day, just as they make little sense today to the majority of 20th century middle-class Christians.

Perhaps he learned it from his mother. Mary, in her Magnificat before Jesus' birth, tells how the Lord "regarded the low estate of his handmaiden" and speaks prophetically of him "filling the hungry with good things, and the rich he has sent empty away" (Luke 1:48, 53). These are a poor woman's words, just as Jesus' instruction to "give to everyone who begs from you" (Luke 6:30) is a saying of the poor, an expression not found in the vocabulary of the rich. He was one of the poor and so he used their words and phrases.

Metamorphosis

In the process of entering God's being, we also enter fully into the complete nature of our humanity, our society and culture. Jesus set us a pattern for cross-cultural ministry when he became a man "and dwelt amongst us, full of grace and truth; we have beheld his glory" (John 1:14).

Being "full of grace" means that Jesus fully entered in and mastered the intricacies of our cultural forms. He spent thirty years learning Aramaic and Jewish culture.

Being "full of truth" means there are elements in his life that supersede all cultures, and refuse to adapt to the evil in any culture. We have "beheld his glory" as he expressed God's culture through the thought-forms and actions of the Jewish soul.

Many people think of cultural change as adjusting to heat (32°C / 90°F) or humidity (98.5%), living on a diet of fish and rice, being called an *Americano,* having to adapt to the daily pattern of *siestas,* traveling in a jeepney, eating at a *carinderia* (a snack shop), or bargaining for a shirt.

These things are initial adjustments, involving some degree of culture stress which, if it is beyond our emotional capacity, could result in culture shock. But such experiences are fun and relatively easy to comprehend compared with the issues of cultural change.

Cultural change is primarily a matter of *inner* change: change not at the level of external behavior (important though this is in becoming "full of grace"), but at the level of our inner emotional responses. Knowledge, study, wisdom, experience, and language are all necessary. It is here that dying to self is critical.

How do I rebuke in a society that knows little direct rebuke? What is my status in a place where status is not based on achievements alone, but on position, wealth, power, age, good looks, and whiteness of face?

As we ask these types of questions, we cannot simply replace our Western culture with Filipino culture. Rather we must evaluate *both* cultures against biblical values—we must move from a Western expression of biblical character to a Filipino expression. No culture is absolute. Only the Scriptures are. The Bible judges all cultures.

Intellectual understanding comes slowly. I can spend days contrasting the culture of New Zealand—"the passionless people" as one author calls us—with Filipino culture, which is certainly not lacking in passion. Change in my emotional responses comes even more slowly, as I move from individualism to group-centeredness, from the Kiwi authoritarian, structure-oriented leadership model to Filipino consensus decision-making, from a male-dominated society to a matriarchal society, from frugality to a celebrating lifestyle, from an egalitarian society (all men are equal) to a traditionally status-oriented society, from achievement-orientation to people-orientation.

Lessons in child-rearing

In living with Ka Emilio, I was in a perfect situation to observe two areas: child-raising patterns (the basis of indigenous training concepts) and family life (the basis of indigenous group structures, social relationships, and value systems).

One interesting feature of Filipino child-raising patterns is that control and discipline are not maintained by *punishment* for violation of principles, but rather by the *presence* of the mother, aunt, or older sister, who constantly limits and molds the child's behavior according to the responses of people around.

One evening I was sitting at the table eating supper. Emy was dramatizing his courtship for me. Little Alma, three years old, was running around.

"Huwag kang malikot," Ate Luz admonished the small boy. This means "don't run around" and also "don't be naughty." To be too active is to be naughty: an active child is difficult to control.

Shame is the critical element. Often I would hear *"Baka, magalit si Viv"* (Watch out, Viv might get angry) as a way of shaming a child into obedience. To make someone angry is a great sin.

Later in life, the same social mechanisms function in the development of ministry and eldership teams: constant sensitivity to the group, molding each other little by little, "shaming" a group member if he oversteps the mark. Groups are very conscious of what onlookers think of the group as a whole, lest they be shamed.

Shock!

Culture shock takes place when cultural stress is beyond our capacity to cope, causing us to react emotionally and irrationally and revert to the immature reactions of childhood. In a sense, you must become a child again—seeing yourself as a child learning the simplest things of life. Culture shock is the result of tension between our prior experience and our current status. It is the result of failure added to failures: failure in bargaining, failure in giving due respect to an official, failure in language, failure in ministry. Our "ego" is suddenly undermined. One morning I jotted:

> Life here is full of failure of cultural adjustment. Failure in saying the right thing, doing the right thing, thinking the right thing. But only in failure comes success. Only in death is life, only in pressing into future failure comes the metamorphosis of cultural adaptation. That's the joy of being a missionary. That is the thrill of mission: walking into death in order to find life—and the knowledge of the One who conquered death.

The culture stress of those months of language study amongst the poor of Lipa City had many components. Knowing of no clear directions, I would have to carve out new models of ministry. Knowing of no group, no organization from which to recruit others to work with the urban poor, I would have to raise up co-laborers. I was used to having a team around me and missed the thrust and parry of activity that had been my lifestyle for years. The uncertainties of mastering the language, of doing anything significant, at times would overwhelm me, only to be pushed back by meditation on such Scriptures as "Wait for the Lord; be strong, and let your heart take courage" (Psalms 27:14).

There is stress relating to other missionaries. The most difficult cultural adjustment was not to Filipino culture but to American. I think it would be true to say that most Kiwis (the nickname for New Zealanders) grow up with an antipathy to American culture for its apparent arrogance. The same appears to be true of most Australian and British people. We grow with a deep nationalism that identifies our egalitarian culture as superior to that of American capitalism and its "man-is-a-machine" administration systems. Many times I had to bring these prejudices before God in repentance. But love covers a multitude of sins. Missionaries of different nationalities need to walk together in forgiving love.

I had to seek consciously the positive aspects of other cultures. From my British heritage, I have learned the importance of being a scholar and a gentleman; from my American brethren I have learned the importance of productivity and achievement; from my Kiwi background how to take life as it comes and to pioneer; from Filipino culture, I have learned how to enjoy life and people.

In time, one comes to a degree of cultural sensitivity. Many missionaries looking back on those first years wish they had taken more time for study of the surrounding culture. The demands of people, leadership roles, and our own personal expectations promote impatience, however, and we jettison the ideal of concentration on culture and language learning needed to become a worthy servant of God, acceptable to him and to the people.

It is a wise "grain" that takes the full time of winter to die— time needed to read, study, think, experiment, and internalize the life of the new culture into which it is being planted.

Finally, we begin to enter into the soul of the people. We begin to speak their soul language and know a little of their soul music. But no matter how far we come, the in-built values in any culture ultimately reject foreigners. This rejection prevents full integration and reminds us that we are strangers and exiles in this world, looking forward to a more permanent dwelling. Such intermittent rejection should also remind us that we will never fully understand another culture—that we are guests in another's "house" and must accept that limitation.

Language study

In becoming man, Jesus took the time to learn our language, to learn our heartbeat. He came walking softly, speaking on our terms in our language.

Initially, language study increases stress by its very monotony, by its constant failure, failure, failure, and by forcing one out to talk with people one does not understand. But as time goes on, the increasing facility for communication provides warmth, laughter, and love. The process of studying the language leads one in a series of supervised cultural learning experiences.

Language study is an emotional life.

An apple and taped vocabulary at five in the morning, chatter with the little boy next door about everything under the sun, five hours of tutoring, a last listen to the tape before sleep, and tomorrow, and tomorrow . . . until March next year. It is a droning air-conditioner punctuated by the humdrum repetition of a phrase, a phrase, a phrase—and the other students' deadpan, weary faces.

Each day begins with a drama. Then mastery of the dialogue and grammar, rote memorizing of the phrases, and finally heading out to practice on friends. In the middle is a break for a snack or a game of table tennis.

By the end of the morning, the class is mentally exhausted. We fail and fail again at language. But there is the thrill of daily becoming more skilled with words, of talking to people, of being able to understand a television program, of preaching for the first time in that language. Finally, freedom begins to come, bringing that same exultant feeling we had when we first learned to whistle, or swim, or tie our shoelaces.

And there is humor! I recall my first day in Tatalon. I had been looking for the pump. *"Nasaan ang bomba?"* (Where is the bomba?), I inquired of a group of ladies. There was silence, then a round of hilarious laughter. I thought *bomba* meant pump. It means a movie star! The ladies still joked with me about it years later.

Executive footwasher

Jesus not only became fully human, learning our language and ways. He not only dwelt amongst the poor. He chose something deeper—an inner dependence of spirit, an inner humility:

> [For] though he was in the form of God.
> [he] did not count equality with God
> a thing to be grasped,
> but emptied himself,
> taking the form of a servant,
> being born in the likeness of men.
> And being found in human form
> he humbled himself
> and became obedient unto death,
> even death on a cross (Philippians 2:6–8)

How easy to live as a poor man; how hard to be a poor man's servant! How easy is external poverty; how hard is poverty of the spirit! External identification must always be matched by inner humility.

The executive sits behind his expensive desk, swinging quietly in his leather chair as the conversation progresses, in-box, out-box, dictaphone, telephone, secretary's clickety-clack, harbor view, air-conditioned room. Perhaps it's you—or is it me?

Secure! Powerful! Wealthy! Proud!

Pride feeds on security; pride feeds on wealth; pride feeds on control and success. My training as an engineer taught me to control, taught me the paths to power, success and efficiency—and taught me pride.

How subtle that pride! These friends—Emy, Luz, Ka Emilio—wished to honor me as a Westerner as I ate with them. They didn't want me to do my share of the physical labor of fetching water. I had to work doubly hard at choosing the lowest place and the most difficult jobs.

One missionary friend came to believe that the honor given him by Filipino friends was his rightful heritage. We must never believe the lie that says we are better than another because we have a different colored face or a fat wallet. We must constantly renounce such flattery. The very heart of identification is communicating to another that he or she, too, is a person of equal worth. We need to actively choose the apparently inefficient way, even to sidestep the seemingly important people, that we might honor the nobodies! Such was Jesus' style.

People's respect and honor must not stem from the color of my skin and my wealth. It must come from the recognition of the Lord within me, that same Lord described by John: "Knowing . . . that he had come from God and was going to God, (he) rose from supper, laid aside his garments, and girded himself with a towel. Then he poured water into a basin, and began to wash the disciples' feet, and to wipe them with the towel with which he was girded" (John 13:3–5).

I heard that one of the world's great religious leaders once washed the feet of twelve old men. For this menial task, he used a pure gold basin! The princes of the church, the men of power, riches, and authority, the international congress on this or that have some small influence on the kingdom. But servants? They are God's strategy.

In dying to ourselves, respect will not come because of a powerful position. It will be because of the power of Christ. That power comes through small acts of humility—the choosing of the lesser place, the less thankful tasks. In Andrew Murray's definition of humility, it is perfect quietness of heart; it is never sore or irritated or disappointed. It is to expect nothing, to wonder at nothing that is done to me, to be at rest when nobody praises me and when I am blamed and despised.

Opposition from missionary friends helped reinforce my commitment to humility. A respected evangelist friend visited me in Ka Emilio's house and over breakfast advised me not to be critical of those who choose a richer lifestyle, since God is impartial. I was tired of the old arguments, so I kept my peace. He pointed out that the inefficiency *of* a lifestyle of poverty would hinder my ministry.

Yet efficiency, too, is a part of us that must die if the gospel is to be preached to the poor. The choice of seeming *inefficiency* is a choice that ultimately brings *effectiveness.* By neglecting our customary patterns of effectiveness, we find our Lord's patterns beginning to manifest themselves—the patterns of humility, of becoming fully human, of identification.

I could only continue in the belief that poverty and humility are both prerequisites to real spiritual power and to a successful ministry. I wrote:

> I easily get wiped out and discouraged unless each day I get that time with God, going over every attitude, meditating on each detail of life and praying over each step forward. If I do not spend that time, I will never have the dependence on God and humility to survive emotionally in this place, nor can God advance his kingdom.

During this time of meditating on these issues and of rejecting traditional mission patterns, the lives of St. Francis Xavier and Francis of Assisi were strong encouragements. For Xavier, poverty was the protection for the religious leader against deterioration into a life of comfort. It secured him from the desire for possessions to which so many monks had succumbed. Both Xavier and Assisi saw poverty as essentially apostolic—it enabled them to serve more freely, to evangelize more effectively.

For Francis of Assisi poverty was his "bride," his chosen "lady." Xavier too loved poverty dearly. He replaced the Franciscan image of "bride" with that of "mother."

It was encouraging also to note how Xavier and his companions learned poverty by experimenting. At times they took nothing on ministry trips; at other times (such as in foreign lands) they took provisions. It encouraged me to persevere.[1]

A renewed passion for the mastery of my inner self began to develop. I was thankful for the seven years of rugged Navigator training in the discipline of thought, developed through Scripture memorization and intensive Bible study. Now the choice of poverty was compelling me to a new level of discipline—the disciplines Jesus gave us in the Sermon of the Mount, the disciplines of spirit. I wrote to a friend:

> The sincerity of our desire to win the world to Christ is measured by the yardstick of self-conquest. Men and women back home ought first to direct their zeal to the conquest of their own relationships, possessions, and delights by the kingdom. You cannot wage war in a dark land, on a dark devil unless the war is first directed against egotism and self-love. For the man of God works frequently from a bed of sickness, in the midst of loneliness and bitterness, and in God we must conquer with joy.
>
> We must expect and delight to share in the sufferings of Christ. Xavier taught that, "failing such a disposition, enthusiasm itself fails. The apostle cannot discharge the rigorous and exacting duties of his office if he becomes embittered by the thought that, at forty, he will be past his prime, by the loneliness

of his wanderings, by the frequent "you are aware that all who are in Asia have deserted me" or "at the first no one stood to my defence." To the Christian, suffering is a delight, for it causes him so much more to become complete. External hardship leads to inner strength. External ease leads to flabbiness of soul.

We are to "train ourselves in godliness." Paul says, speaking figuratively, "I pommel my body and subdue it, lest after preaching to others I myself should be disqualified." This joy, this ability to face suffering and utilize it for good, is the result of hard discipline in training our minds in small things.

There can be little success without the daily memorizing of the Word of God until hundreds and indeed thousands of verses control our thinking. I can well remember several godly men, about whose lives I have noticed an unusually toughened holiness. They were men of the memorized word, men of a holy mind.

Boxed in by humanity

Imitatio Cristi is an old phrase of the church that describes a life of identification with the poor, of incarnating Christ. Choosing to lead such a life leads us deep into the nature of Jesus' deity. Jesus identified himself with the poor. But he never was *identical*. Though he could classify himself as a poor man, as one of the anaw, he was always God. He had two natures.

The Western missionary has a similar duality of nature. No matter how simply we live, we are always rich. We have traveled. We have a hundred rich friends. We are educated. And, if we are white, we cannot change our bone structure or skin color to identify fully with the people.

To be poor among the poor, we must recognize this duality. Incarnation is not becoming hopeless among the hopeless. It is, instead, to become involved in the poor man's sufferings and lifestyle to show that in Jesus alone is hope. It is to bring the riches of rich friends, our resources of wealth and education and power, to affect the needs of the poor.

Jesus' incarnation was not that of becoming a malnourished beggar, but becoming fully human in the context of inhumanity. Identification is not becoming destitute, but demonstrating, by actions of love and deeds of spiritual power, the fullness of Christ.

We must beware of overemphasizing Jesus' poverty. Though he became poor, he ate daily, wore a finely woven robe, and grew up with a skilled trade as a *tekton* (a cross between a carpenter, cabinetmaker, and stone mason—a skilled job, perhaps equivalent today to that of an engineer or architect). He loved to celebrate and freely went to rich men's houses. He and the twelve disciples gave to a class of poor who were even poorer than themselves.

Though at times, like Paul, we may choose a greater life of poverty and suffering for the gospel, we need to avoid the extremes of ascetic poverty of Xavier and Assisi. We need to know the limitations of chosen poverty.

The fear of economic insecurity

Choosing poverty raised another fear. From my study of poverty, I knew the inevitability of the poor getting poorer. I was afraid because the choice of poverty seems more costly than it would have been in Jesus' day. It is one thing to choose voluntarily a poverty from which I can move. But if I do not develop the computer skills for which my engineering training prepared me, I may lose my options. I may become one of the *involuntary poor.*

Rather than immerse myself completely into a life of poverty, I wanted to hang on to both worlds—to become bicultural. And indeed that is the life I have ended up living—the life of a poor rich man.

I've chosen to maintain my skills in one world for use when needed, while living in the other world of poverty the majority of the time. So too, the Son of God moved from the realm of infinite riches to his life of poverty. So, too, we find St. Francis Xavier, when confronted by the intransigence of the *Bonzes* of Japan, dressing up in all his glory as a *Papal Nuncio* and visiting them in state. His reason? To gain freedom to work on his status as one of the sons of the rich to unite the rich and poor in his own divided city of Assisi.

The problem is the motivation behind living a bicultural lifestyle. Fear is the complete antithesis of Jesus' command to simplicity:

> Therefore I tell you, do not be anxious about your life, what you shall eat, nor about your body, what you shall put on. . . . Fear not, little flock, for it is your Father's good pleasure to give you the kingdom. Sell your possessions, and give alms. (Luke 12:22, 32–33)

To help the poor, it is reasonable for us to oscillate back into a wealthier lifestyle at times. This, however, must not be for personal protection. We must not shrink back from the high calling of the poor Master to a life of external poverty and inner humility. It must be always for the sake of these poor. And in all this, he promises to provide for our needs.

But we must be realistic about the limitations of our humanity. At one stage I made a list of these limitations:

(a) The need for room and time to study, to pray, to sleep.

I remember the first time I slept in the same bed with another co-worker. I did not sleep all night! For people who grow up sleeping on the same mat with their family, it is natural to share a bed. Indeed, it is strange to most Filipinos that a Westerner should wish to sleep in a private bedroom.

Fortunately, as a university student, I had learned to study in the midst of all sorts of noise and people. But at the same time, every "monk" needs his own cell for prayer and study.

(b) Limited by food needs

Each day Ate Luz would boil my water, since my stomach had no resistance to amoeba, fungus, worms, or bacteria. Even so, because it is hard to boil water on a wood fire, I soon contracted all four.

Having grown up on meat, I found it difficult to live on the staple diet of fish and rice. We worked out an arrangement so that I could eat some meat each day.

(c) Limited by my intellectual need for time to think.

I am not only called to the poor. I am called to lead men and women. And such leadership requires mastery of complex issues. Much of my motivation to pioneer comes from the exploration of ideas, of theology.

(d) Limited by my emotional need for time out of poverty to cope with culture shock.

One weekend a month I would return to Manila to fetch my mail and to enjoy some company with some other missionaries. Often I would watch a good

British movie or a TV program to throw my mind back into Western culture.

(e)   Limited by my achievement needs, built up through years of living and mastering an achievement-oriented culture.

(f)   Limited by my needs to interface with my own culture through correspondence and typing.

(g)   Limited by my own quietness, my seriousness, and directness.

At times I found I needed to retreat inside myself, away from the exuberance and display of emotions that make Filipinos such a fun-loving people.

Which Jesus?

A further complicating factor in Imitatio Cristi, the lifestyle of imitating Christ, is that Jesus had several lifestyles.

He lived in a stable home and had a stable childhood. Then came a long time of maturing, training, and working. He had times of withdrawal, times of mission, times of ministry.

The missionary in the slum also needs to be a quick-change artist from one lifestyle to another—within the same day being a poor man laboring in the slums, a successful missionary interacting with rich donors, an evangelist preaching to sinners, and a mystic taking time out to be alone with God.

After many months of musing, I came to the simple conclusion that I could call individuals, or couples without children, to live among the urban poor, provided they had a good toilet, control over cooking food, control over boiling water, a day of rest outside the slums each week, and a companion.

But what about those with children? Could they have an effective ministry to the poor? There is no simple answer. Raising children in the midst of poverty is a difficult task. To work from outside a community is a difficult, perhaps impossible task, yet could prove effective. John Wesley succeeded in his ministry by living outside the communities where he preached. Those with support roles, such as administration or the development of economic projects, could certainly do so from the outside of the slum communities.

Even those living within the slum communities will spend much time out of the communities working to obtain justice, political assistance, or economic aid, and to take time needed for rest, retreat, or recuperation.

Perhaps the critical issue is the heart commitment of a couple to identify with the poor. Where there is a will, there is a way!

Next steps

As I struggled to identify with the poor and grow in the knowledge of God, an inner certainty began to fill me. I knew I was standing for a central truth the Lord was speaking to the church. I knew that God would raise up a band of Filipinos to meet social, economic, and physical needs. And I had a growing sense that he would lead out a band of men and women from other countries to work among the poor. I began to think through the basis for a new mission structure from the suburbs of the West to the slums of the East.

But it was time for the Lord to teach me the next step. And as usual, it wasn't what I expected.

Stricken with a bad case of amoeba, I had to leave Ka Emilio's house for a friend's middle-class Manila home. The doctor mistakenly prescribed the wrong medicine, affecting my heart. I was forced to stay in bed for two months. I changed doctors, but by that time my liver was affected.

As I slowly regained my health, I continued language study in Manila. At the same time, I was asked to bring together the leaders of Bible studies for professionals throughout Manila. Although the Lord may not have wanted me to leave my language study and his clear call to serve the poor, he used the experience to transform my view of discipleship.

NOTES
1. The best motivational books I have found on these men are: Pascual Oiz, S. J., Saint Francis Xavier, *The Mystical Progress of the Apostle* (Bandra, Bombay: St Paul Press Training School, 1976), and Sabatier, P. and J. M. Sweney, *The Road to Assisi: The Essential Biography of St Francis* (Paraclete Press, 2003).

Chapter Five

Paved with Good Intentions
INADEQUATE CONCEPTS OF DISCIPLESHIP

The process of multiplying disciples began with Jesus. It was central to all he did. In his final prayer before he was taken to the cross, he told his Father he had "accomplished the work which thou gavest me to do" (John 17:4).

He then reiterated these accomplishments. They were chiseled into the lives of twelve men: "I have given *them* thy words . . . *they* have believed . . . I am praying for *them* . . . I have guarded *them* . . . for *their* sake I consecrate myself " (John 17:8–19, emphasis added).

Jesus commanded his disciples to "go . . . and make disciples" (Matthew 28:19). The passion for a lifestyle of disciple making was *his* passion.

In New Zealand, I grew up with a close-knit band of men and women who shared a demanding dream. We had a drive and zeal for one thing: to make disciples and bring the world to the knowledge of our Lord. We were confident of our plan, sure of our steps, fully committed to our methodology.

But in order to prepare me to reach the poor, God decided to shatter that dream, that passion, that zeal. He then restored them all, reshaped according to his model of discipleship. He did it very simply through a destitute woman.

"Brod, pahingi?"

She came to me after I had spent several hours of prayer in a beautiful Catholic chapel.

I went there often. It was one place where I could be reasonably alone from the ever-probing, demanding, laughing eyes of Manila's crowds.

The walls were open, looking out onto green grass and great old trees—a pleasant sight in a city of dust and concrete.

The hours of quiet had left me feeling religious, holy, and together again, ready for another week of action. I walked beneath the restful trees towards the bus stop.

"Brod . . . brod!"

I felt the voice, rather than heard it.

"Brod, brod!" I looked behind me and a shudder ran through me, though my body betrayed nothing. Never had I seen such an ugly face. I felt ashamed at my response. She came hesitatingly to me and I waited for her request. There must be a request.

"Brod, brod, pahingi twenty pesos!" (Brother, brother, please give me twenty pesos!).

She spoke softly and urgently, but uncertainly and with shame, unlike the professional, brazen beggars. Her face was pockmarked all over. Not the usual beautiful honey brown, but the color of a pink powder puff, covered in protrusions and hollows. The child on her hip was obviously very sick.

A wild light in her eyes indicated desperation had overtaken shame and she said more insistently, *"Brod, pahingi fifty pesos."*

She reached out to grasp my arm. Inwardly, I cowed back. But I knew that Jesus would not have pulled away.

"Bakit, mare? Ang bang problema?" (Why mother, what's your problem?) I asked, knowing as I asked that the humiliation she would suffer in answering would require me to give.

Her child was about be hospitalized, she explained. She herself was nearing death. She was afraid to die while he was there. I thought of the one hundred pesos in my wallet.

Suddenly her boldness overcame all her reserve.

"Brod, pahingi one hundred pesos!" With a fleeting thought of lunch and my bus fare, I gave her the one hundred pesos.

She left as softly and as quickly as she had come, embarrassed and murmuring, "God bless you."

Shattered discipleship

I walked on, outwardly looking as I had before I had met her. But inside, a battle was going on. I had spent years of my life teaching a "spiritual" concept of discipleship. Suddenly, that concept came face-to-face with a poor woman, a child, and her haunting pleas. I had given total commitment to a demanding dream. Now this dream was inadequate—only half good, a half-truth. I had been zealous for my cause, but my cause itself had been imperfect.

I felt shattered; unable to cope. I saw the half-faces, like Picasso's half-masks, reaching out to me across Manila like nightmares. I was filled with horror as I realized that I had been betrayed—that I had betrayed myself and in doing so had betrayed others.

We had taught boldly and been taught thoroughly that discipleship was individualistic and "spiritual"—that our responsibility was to teach, to preach, and to disciple (i.e., to impart truths about prayer, the Bible, devotional life, and the Holy Spirit, and to "save souls"). We had commended non-involvement in the great social issues of our time. In answer to the cries of the pockmarked poor, we had turned our backs, asking, "Am I my brother's keeper?"

That question reverberated in the depths of my soul as I hurried, dazed, from appointment to appointment. I saw a mother sleeping in the street in her little mobile cart, a man with putrid, festering sores begging for help, another wasted with the yellow color of a destroyed liver. Over and over again I wondered, *Where was the social component to my discipleship?*

I had to admit that my years of teaching and preaching a "spiritual" discipleship had been misguided. Although friends might reject me as having lost my single-mindedness and total commitment to evangelism, I would have to repent and seek a Jesus-style discipleship. I had to go back to the Scriptures and find a discipleship that brought together all of life—social, economic, political, spiritual—under the Lordship of Jesus Christ, a discipleship that dealt with today's injustices.

I had never heard an exposition about the biblical responsibility to transform the social institutions of a city and secure provision for a pockmarked widow. I had never been taught how to help a poor squatter landlady who was oppressing those yet poorer as they rented her squatter home.

Discipleship means that disciples have to find Jesus' answers for the exploited factory workers, and how the poor should respond to the moneylenders (who demand their six pesos tomorrow for the five they give you today). The Bible has much to teach about what we should do with such problems of oppression.

Discipleship also has to deal with the slums themselves, as well as with the displaced peasants who cannot cope in an industrial society. It has to deal with the animism and spirit worship that still clutch at society.

Disciplemaking is the transmission of life-to-life. It is caught, not taught. It is a fire that breeds fire. It is not a method, a program, nor even the teaching and preaching of the Word of God—though all of these are involved. Disciplemaking is God's love being poured out through one life into another, until the second life catches that love. It is faith imparted by one to another. It is an absolute commitment to the Word of God, communicated in the midst of ministry pressures as men and women co-labor together.

I had given a woman one hundred pesos. But she had asked for my life. Sitting on a rock in the middle of a park, I made a life-long commitment to bring what has come to be known as "holistic discipleship" to the masses of Asia's cities.

Culturally appropriate discipleship

The first step in moving from "spiritual" to holistic discipleship is the process of adapting Western models of discipleship.

The missionary who wishes to make disciples must go deep into the soul of the people. A disciple of Christ is one who follows the disciplines of Christ. Many think of these disciplines as the scheduling of set times of prayer, Bible reading, and so on. But Christ gave little teaching on such things (except to avoid parading them). His are the disciplines of the inner person, the disciplines of the Beatitudes and the Sermon on the Mount— qualities such as humility, meekness, and peacemaking. These involve the transformation of the inner soul of a person. That inner soul is deeply molded by one's culture, a culture that may include values close to those of Christ, as well as others directly opposed to him.

The perception of which values need transformation, at which stage of Christian development, and how this can be accomplished requires a deep understanding of any culture. The role of the missionary working with an indigenous movement is to understand these forces, acting as a catalyst to such changes within the movement's leadership.

Many of us have a low view of disciplemaking, considering it as imparting basic Bible doctrine. We reduce concepts of discipleship into programs and packages. Programs and packages may be an important component of ministry within a specific sub-cultural grouping, but they are not transferable to other cultures. The resultant lack of cultural relevance is seen in reproduced Western church structures, Western church buildings, Western worship patterns, and Western Bible school training.

I was fortunate. Gene Tabor and other leaders of the REACH movement had succeeded in re-thinking an American pattern of ministry from within a Filipino cultural framework. Few other groups have been as successful in this process. I could learn first-hand from my Filipino brothers and sisters about culturally suitable discipleship.

Ministry growth

God was blessing this contextualized ministry. Where we thought in terms of reaching whole social groups—whole offices, whole families, or *barkadas*—people came to Christ.

What does a missionary working in partnership with Filipinos among Manila's middle class do? I usually preached two or three times weekly and enjoyed double-teaming with my leader who had responsibility for the development of the whole movement. This is the role I enjoy most in the ministry—supporting another, complementing, encouraging. It was a challenging task, requiring a dexterity far more demanding than being the kingpin and a greater depth of emotional maturity. I was encouraged to see the result of a similar supportive relationship from my earlier years in Manila. (There were now several disciplemakers in the first church I had been involved in planting.)

We established monthly fellowships for different groups of people in Manila—a college group, a Makati group (the business center of Manila), a couples' group, and a social workers' fellowship. Requests for help kept coming from pastors, students, and professionals.

A pastor was excited about the idea of teaching his church how to have family devotions. It was the first time he had ever thought to have prayer times with his elders. There was a real breakthrough. Family devotions began to become a regular part of church life.

The ministry involved extensive counseling and training. I met weekly with ten to twenty people. I traveled on weekends with others on the staff to minister to students in the outlying agricultural universities. We put together manuals on the basics of Christian growth and follow-up for these three-day trips. The men who made up the teams during these trips are now leaders of these ministries.

The climax of my work with the professionals and in the wider ministry of the REACH movement came with the opportunity to lead a training program for 194 leaders from the core groups of each of the thirteen agricultural university ministries.

One day, we split program trainees into groups of fifteen and sent them out to the barrios to "preach the gospel to the poor." Each group developed a drama, some special musical items and testimonies, while one of the men preached. Over 100 came to Christ. One of the men was so excited after this experience of preaching to the poor that the next month he gathered together a team to preach in a slum.

First steps

This process of culturally appropriate discipleship can be seen in the story of Manuel.

When I first met him, Manuel was a final year college student. He was an easy person to relate to. He invited me to a delicious supper of stuffed fish, rice and other dishes served by his family. After supper, we sat down together and discussed question by question a Bible study entitled "Assurance of Salvation."

Even in this first study, culture affected the content of the follow-up. Three factors were constantly in mind as we discussed the passages.

First, Catholicism has used biblical terms, but given them different meanings. The result is that, for many, it takes weeks for the gospel to become clear.

Second, many in poor societies have grown up in broken family relationships. For such it may take months to establish a clear picture of God the Father as just, merciful, dependable, and loving.

Third, since the basic culture is rooted in animism, basic follow-up begins by confronting a worldview of a pantheon of good and evil spirits.

Group or person-to-person discipleship?

In the highly structured, time-conscious, impersonal culture of the West, "person-to-person" discipleship is most effective. This involves, among other things, a weekly meeting of an hour to an hour-and-a-half for sharing in Bible study and prayer, and reviewing the memorized Word. It is an extremely powerful technique in an individualistic culture.

But in a traditional, group-oriented, personal, creative, emotive society, with a time consciousness that is cyclic and event-oriented and a keen sense of the occasion, such a methodology is disastrous.

Personal discipling is an extremely threatening methodology to someone who has grown up rarely being alone—and usually never alone (unless married) with only one other person. In Asia, personal relationships are expressed by accompanying someone somewhere, in assisting someone to do something, or in attending a family function.

The principle of transferring truth in the context of a deep personal relationship is universal, but its specific cultural form is not cross-cultural. The ancient biblical principles of discipleship remain unchanged, but they are expressed in different cultural forms, with an appropriate fit between biblical and contemporary culture.

I believed that Manuel would come through to discipleship only if we reached his *barkada* (a group of close-knit friends) around him. I prayed for the opportunity to meet them.

The next time I visited Manuel, his drinking mates were sitting around the table with him. He was watching me carefully to see how I would cope, to see if I could relate. He asked his sister to serve me a cup of tea, and we joked our way through numerous introductions. Then the questions began to come.

Half-drunk men are painfully realistic. We talked a lot about that unusual person, Jesus Christ, and about trust.

"I trust no one, not even my closest friend!" declared one of the barkada looking around at his closest friends. He was a Muslim. His father had three wives, and he had grown up in an atmosphere of distrust. We talked of Jesus and his forgiveness, but the Muslim was far too drunk to consider trusting the man from Galilee.

After a while I took my leave, having made friends for myself but not yet for the Master.

But the following week, Manuel brought his girl friend Celia and two other friends to a Bible study in my home. My cooking was not up to such an occasion, so Celia cooked while we discussed how we could know God's forgiveness.

The next week, Henry, one of Manuel's friends, was high on drugs during the study. Two days later, he decided to leave his home, so he brought his belongings over with him to my place. We discussed the Word of God about obedience to parents and sent him back home. Celia was not yet a Christian, so I took Celia and Manuel out for a meal in the restaurant in the park. We discussed how to get Henry off drugs, and then I explained to Celia how she, too, could know she has eternal life. She happily accepted it.

Animism

Manuel told me about the problem he was having memorizing Scripture. He would sit in his room, but every time he took out his verse pack to memorize Scripture, the lights in the room would die. When he put the verses away, the lights would return.

Some years before, we had been praying for his older sister to be released from demonic attacks.

In such a context, what are the first steps in disciplemaking? Is not basic follow-up to confront the occult powers, to transform the people's worldview, showing clearly the difference between the kingdom of God and the kingdoms of this world? Some months later, we went up to his room and prayed, commanding the spirit to leave.

But to free Manuel and his sister, the whole family had to renounce any dealings with the spirit world, including putting away their Catholic idols—statues of the Virgin and of the saints.

Many of the leading church-planters in the Philippines have come to a position of avoiding direct confrontation with Catholicism, preferring to teach new believers about the Bible and Christian discipleship. Believers very quickly cease praying to Mary upon learning the power of prayer. At times idols are publicly burnt, but mostly they are quietly taken down and hidden, destroyed, or, if family heirlooms, given to others in the family.

In the same way, as it takes months, even years, for believers to cease their drinking, gambling, and immorality (oscillating between these and prayer and Bible study meetings), it takes some time for believers to assemble together into worship. When they do begin to attend regularly, demonstrating a clear stability of commitment and life, it appears wise to baptize believers. Earlier baptism is seen by the family only as a sign of conversion to Protestantism, not as a sign of repentance from sin, severely limiting any further evangelism among relatives and neighbors.

Cultural leadership patterns

In developing a leadership team for Bible studies, I needed to learn numerous other cultural values. Among them were the role of women, consensus decision-making, and group centeredness.

Filipino women are held in higher respect than their counterparts in other cultures. In the Philippines, women run 80 percent of businesses. Men are the head, the ultimate authority, but women do the real decision-making. Women usually handle family finances.

When I began, I tried to develop key men for the management of the work. That was a mistake, a trespassing on the woman's role. The men's role was to teach and preach—to be the figureheads. The women were to organize and determine where, when, and how.

A second change needed in my leadership style was in the process of decision-making. In the Philippines, the leadership team sits and discusses for hours. The leader should sit and listen, gently feeling for the consensus of the group. If a consensus is not reached in a meeting, no decision can be made.

Further discussion may create that critical harmony necessary for decision. Harmony with others, with God, and with nature are crucial components in most Asian cultures, in contrast to our own culture, where achievement is the ultimate and often only point of evaluation.

Hours of small talk, joking, and engaging in apparently "time-wasting" conversation are critical factors in the Filipino mind for creating the right atmosphere of freedom, harmony, and unity.

Planning, too, is developed on a different model. Filipinos, it seems, easily perceive the *ultimate* goal, the glorious vision of a brilliant future. The implications for the present are deduced from this, the group collectively deeply committed to its realization.

Intermediate goals may be verbalized, but the concrete steps required for their fulfillment are not spelled out in case they restrict the creativity that is the driving force behind Filipino achievements. This is quite a contrast to the highly structured planning models of the West, with their emphasis on pre-planning at every step.

Economic repentance

As my view of discipleship changed, my friends in New Zealand were also adjusting. They understood enough missions theory to appreciate cross-cultural deviations from the norm of disciplemaking, but what was most disconcerting for them— and threatening—was the economic implications of holistic discipleship.

While I lived with Ka Emilio, I had already been meeting some small economic and social needs. Four rabbits happily played outside the window of my room. I experimented to see if these might be a way of supplementing my regular intake of meat. I would go jogging each morning, collecting grass and *ipil-ipil* leaves for them on the way. Eventually I concluded that rabbits were too complex a husbandry project for most poor families.

For years, the REACH movement had a deep commitment to meeting socio-economic needs. This had been demonstrated symbolically in a pig farm. The six-week-old piglets were given to poor families who raised them to seven months on food scraps, and then sold them for a small sum to supplement their income. The farm had a training center where educated Filipinos could learn to work with their hands. It was also a center for other economic projects.

We spent time and effort to recruit money from Tear Fund for an airlift pump developed by a Canadian friend for the farm. He believed it would lower the price of the average farmer's pump to one-tenth. It was a demonstration of our commitment to small scale, appropriate technology—projects at the technical and economic levels of the people.

After writing a few thoughts home to New Zealand on these economic projects, I received some letters asking if perhaps I had moved from my commitment to evangelism as the thrust of mission. I sought to answer these comments honestly, communicating my growing understanding. They served, as letters normally do, to confuse. I wrote:

I have begun to realize how much our Western culture has molded my view of the Scriptures, how in most areas of our lives we compartmentalize: the social is not the spiritual is not the economic. We have a great divide in our thinking which can be illustrated thus:

$$\frac{Spiritual\ issues\ =\ religion}{Social\text{-}economic\text{-}political\ issues\ =\ life}$$

But the Scriptures are not Western; they are Eastern. They see life as a whole; they are holistic. Discipleship involves the spiritual, i.e. our relationship to God. However, even in the great commission, Jesus includes social and economic repentance along with proclamation to preach. He tells us not only to "go, make disciples" but to "teach them to *observe* all" that he had commanded (Matthew 28:19). Observance involves action. The action is evidenced socially, economically, even politically:

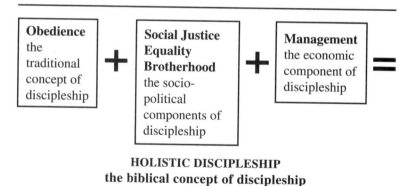

HOLISTIC DISCIPLESHIP
the biblical concept of discipleship

One evening during this time I gave a talk on repentance. I mentioned John the Baptist's demand: "He who has two coats, let him share with him who has none; and he who has food, let him do likewise" (Luke 3:11).

As I spoke, I was struck by the fact that I had never before spoken of economic repentance when I had been preaching the gospel. The repentance I had spoken of had been purely in spiritual terms. From this time on my preaching would define repentance economically, spiritually, socially, and, where necessary, politically. It transformed my evangelism.

A development of the bridge diagram we had often used to portray the gospel now looked like this:

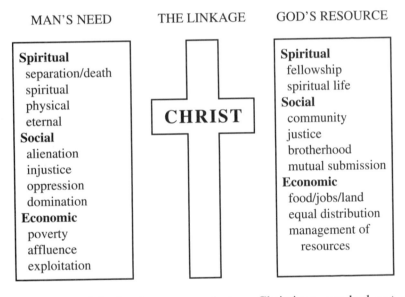

MAN'S NEED	THE LINKAGE	GOD'S RESOURCE
Spiritual		**Spiritual**
separation/death		fellowship
spiritual		spiritual life
physical	**CHRIST**	**Social**
eternal		community
Social		justice
alienation		brotherhood
injustice		mutual submission
oppression		**Economic**
domination		food/jobs/land
Economic		equal distribution
poverty		management of
affluence		resources
exploitation		

Jesus might be the answer, but as Christians, we had not been asking the right questions. Western notions of the gospel and discipleship were irrelevant in the Two-Thirds World except to the upper- and middle-class, whose problems were primarily psychological and emotional needs.

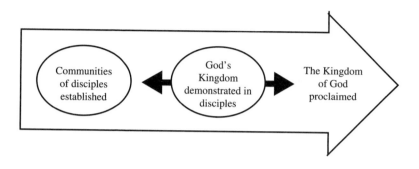

Mission and the gospel

What, then, are our social, economic, and political responsibilities as disciples of Christ? The following responsibilities are commonly thought of as "disciple-making":

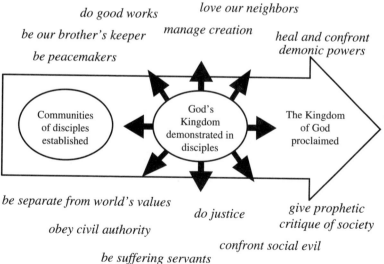

These are primary to all we do, but the Scriptures add the following ways we are to use to influence the world—as salt keeps meat from rotting and light expels darkness.

To these general principles, we may add specific commands regarding social, economic, and political action:

- Speak up for the poor and needy
- Feed the hungry
- Protect widows
- Care for orphans
- Visit prisoners
- Clothe the destitute
- House the homeless
- Give to the poor
- Uphold the rights of the oppressed
- Look after aliens and refugees

Our mission as Christians is primarily to proclaim the truth about God, but we are also to live in the world. Expressing God's life in us involves all of these other factors. We are to be "our brother's keeper;" we are "to manage creation;" we are to "do justice." This is the context in which God's kingdom is proclaimed. All of the commands listed above are parts of our mission as we await the return of our Lord.

Free at last

Our thinking had moved from a Western "spiritual" concept of discipleship to a culturally adapted one, and then to a holistic discipleship. But there was one more step in my search before God could illuminate a theology and strategy for ministry to the urban poor.

Discipleship had been the theme of my life as it is a dominant theme in the Scriptures, but I was gradually becoming uneasy about making it the center of my theology. I had begun to reject the dispensational view which divided biblical history into a series of dispensations, in such a way that (though this is never stated) God changes tactics and character in each dispensation. The Old Testament is relegated to irrelevancy by stating its dispensation. Similarly much of Jesus' teaching becomes obsolete. What is left as important is the "spiritual" teaching of the apostle Paul. Even the apostolic dispensation is considered finished, and with it miracles, signs, and prophetic gifts.

My search culminated one day with explosive illumination— like walking into a floodlit room.

A theology for the poor

I was sitting in a class on the theological perspectives of community development.[1] As Dr. William Dyrness mapped out God's interventions (a community development term) in history (a theological starting point), God intervened! Suddenly, I saw the universal biblical theme around which all of life as well as ministry to the poor could be integrated. It was the greatness, the fullness, the unity of the kingdom of God in the Scriptures and the immutable, unchanging nature of God himself.

I studied how the economic principles of the kingdom were first expressed in the life of Israel, in the life of the Church. I saw that God's economics, though expressed in different contexts, do not change from age to age, but are universal! The politics of God are also universal. His truth was unchanging.[2]

In a flash, the Spirit of God showed me the basis for a theology of developing movements among squatters. My excitement knew no limits. I devoured article after article, verse after verse, and worked eighteen hours a day on the task. My years of searching and questioning had, at last, found a focal point. I now needed time to work back from this focal point and develop a total theology for reaching Asia's squatters.

Eric Hoffer points out that popular movements begin with people of words—the *intelligentsia* who capture the feeling, the mood of the times, and bring it to the notice of the people.[3]

It was such a time in Manila—a time to forge the foundations for a ministry to the squatters from amongst the intellectuals. I sensed that my role, as a foreigner, was to identify the season we were in, recognize God's purpose for the national church, and serve it with all my energy. Within a few days God had enabled the writing of a 40-page article entitled "Christian Perspective on Development Philosophies." It sought to integrate various biblical material on the kingdom of God, the poor, economics, and the realities of present Filipino social conditions.

To some, such academic study may seem meaningless. But thought must precede action. Having broken the bonds of a tightly defined theological system, I needed to establish a new basis for mission. Others could follow—and develop new approaches—if the biblical basis was clear.

A clearly articulated philosophy of poverty and mission was necessary for the government as well. As regular reports were made on my activities in the slums, it was essential that I be able to define my position. The word, I knew, would be passed on to the appropriate authorities. Discipleship is always being ready to give a reason for the hope that is in you! (1 Peter 3:15)

"When you first came, I thought you were a Marxist worker," one of the community leaders would tell me in Tatalon. She was quite suspicious because Marxists had entered Tatalon before. They even had given scholarships to people and worked with the Catholic priests.

I had just explained to another friend in her presence how, as Christians, we wanted to put the control of production and exporting into the hands of the poor—to avoid letting the rich gain control of the economic projects, and to develop cottage industries. But unlike the Marxists, we did not intend to use our economic projects to buy people for Christianity. What we wanted was to assist those who *already* had spiritual life to become stable economically, so they could be relieved from peer-group pressures and from personally destructive behavior like gambling, drunkenness, adultery, and drug addiction.

As an extra bonus, academic mastery of issues relating to politics, economics, and the poor also gave entrance to social workers, community workers, religious leaders, and academics in the upper class. Many key laborers among the poor would come from this group.

Theology in partnership

Twelve theologians from across Asia spent a year studying issues of poverty. Other Filipino evangelical Christians voiced their theologies of community development. It was important to keep in touch with these mainstreams of prophetic witness in the church. Proverbs tells us "in the abundance of counselors is wisdom." The work among the poor grew from such counselors on the cutting edge of Filipino theology.

One of these was Pastor Johnny, the leader of a church we had been involved in establishing some years earlier. Early one morning, as the dawn glowed from pink to blue, we met in the park. We discussed how Jesus' ethical teaching on right relationships leads into Paul's theology of economic and social responsibility. Then we talked through a strategy for work among the poor.

A number of social workers were involved in Bible studies. We sought to draw them together to discuss the biblical basis of social work. Professors had taught them the empty shell of humanistic social work, but they had not yet been able to fully integrate their work with their faith. Some were trapped into doing social work without a biblical base. Discipleship had affected their personal lives in areas of prayer and Bible study, but they wanted it to become the heart of their work. These social workers had already begun to bring significant biblical reforms into government and aid agencies.

Over several weeks during the same period, six other graduates and I met together for a series of studies on the economic implications of discipleship. We discussed issues such as creating work, earning money, caring for the environment, being effective managers of finance, and discovering the responsibilities of the rich to the poor.

Out of these and other discussions, we produced a booklet entitled "Finances and the Kingdom of God" and a number of one-day seminars.

The major components of the theology behind our squatter movement were now on paper. The next phase of ministry was to clearly map out a strategy for the work.

NOTES

1. See Bryant Myers, *Walking with the Poor* (MARC, 1998), for some theology and principles of community transformation.
2. Later published in *Let the Earth Rejoice* (Wipf & Stock Publishers, 1998). Perhaps the best portrayal of the biblical theology of the kingdom of God is George Eldon Ladd, *The Gospel of the Kingdom* (Wipf & Stock Publishers, 1999).
3. Eric Hoffer, *The True Believer* (Harper and Row, Reissued edition 1989).

Chapter Six

To Have or Not to Have?

ECONOMICALLY JUST LIFESTYLES

Disciplemaking is a commitment of one life to another through thick and thin. But since I was not called to these professionals, I could not give my heart to them. I could not be a true pastor, and true disciplemaking could not really occur. All I could do was to set a framework, a structure, and handle the problems as they occurred.

The office Bible studies continued to multiply; the university groups began to come together; a graduate group began at the University of the Philippines; several pastors were asking for help. The ministry grew from seventy to a hundred professionals and college students. And God was giving freedom in my preaching after five years of hard discipline developing story-telling skills and crafting sermons.

But the call of the poor still beat relentlessly in my mind. I was compelled by an inner drive. I must take the gospel to the poor. All my creative energy must be directed towards the poor, the needy, and the broken.

But there would be a cost. What would happen to the relationships with my middle-class co-laborers as I sought to involve them among the poor? How could I involve the middle-class and rich in the needs of the poor? What lifestyle is appropriate for them to live? What models could I use from the past?

Substance and simplicity

Job and Abraham are interesting examples of rich men with a deep commitment to the poor. Both were patriarchs, men of great social standing and influence, living at a time when society was built around a clan structure. Abraham was a man committed to simplicity of lifestyle. Though he had great wealth, he employed it wisely to support his hundreds of dependents (a model for factory owners!). Though he knew how to build cities, having grown up in Ur of the Chaldees, he chose to live simply in a tent. Hebrews tells us: "By faith, he sojourned in the land of promise, as in a foreign land, living in tents with Isaac and Jacob, heirs with him of the same promise. For he looked forward to the city which has foundations whose builder and maker is God" (Hebrews 11:9–10).

Such men can be used to minister to the poor. Abraham established a pattern that is consistent throughout the Scriptures: "The blessing of the Lord makes rich and he adds no sorrow with it" (Proverbs 10:22). Yet those who have wealth are not to live luxuriously but simply, "to be rich in good deeds, liberal and generous" because "the love of money is the root of all evils" (1 Timothy 6:6–8, 10, 18).

In the Scriptures, greed (or covetousness) and excessive luxury are sins as bad as immorality or adultery (Ephesians 5:3–5). Indeed we are not even to have lunch with a brother who is greedy (1 Corinthians 5:11).

If we want to live out a gospel of justice and grace, we must see that living a life of luxury is collaborating with injustice. Piety and luxury cannot co-exist. Living luxuriously in the midst of poverty is a denial of justice: "If anyone has the world's goods and sees his brother in need, yet closes his heart against him, how does God's love abide in him?" (1 John 3:17).

To be obedient to this command surely means that nobody should have excessively more than others. The poor should be uplifted, the rich brought low, and equality should result. (Though clearly we don't keep giving till we too become destitute, for then we only add ourselves to the problem.)

Pastor Jun, Milleth, and children

Pastor Jun and his household: wife, son, mother, sister, and brother

Aling Nena (right), Eleanor (her daughter), and Metzai (left)

Pastor Jun teaching about getting rid of works from the soul

Viv Grigg's home: up the stairs, first on the left

Outside the house: venue for the first Bible studies

A section of Tatalon: 14,500 people per square mile

Squatter homes: erected from any available plywood and galvanized iron

And clearly there is a need for some men to have capital, as Abraham had capital. But we must use it to benefit the workers, as Abraham used it to benefit his people.

Job, the greatest of all patriarchs of the East, also had great capital. He too used it to benefit his people. In his justifications, Job describes how to be a godly rich man:

> I delivered the poor (ani) who cried,
> and the fatherless who had none to help him . . .
> I caused the widow's heart to sing for joy.
> I put on righteousness, and it clothed me;
> my justice was like a robe and turban.
> I was eyes to the blind, and feet to the lame.
> I was a father to the poor (ebyon),
> and I searched out the cause of him
> whom I did not know.
> I broke the fangs of the unrighteous,
> and made him drop his prey from his teeth.
> (Job 29:12–17)

Rich people are to live simply and use their capital to benefit the poor. This is justice. For a Western missionary or a Christian businessman to live otherwise is a great evil.

The poor have an intuitive knowledge about such issues. They know it is unjust that I am a rich man and they are poor. Of course everyone, rich and poor, knows that riches are a gift from God and that sin is a cause of poverty. But the poor man of understanding knows more than a rich man who is wise in his own eyes. He knows it is often the sins of oppression, exploitation, and injustice committed in the name of "fair profit" that have made him poor.

But justice is not to live in equal *destitution* with the destitute. Justice for Jesus was to live humbly, simply, without excess, and share whatever he had with those around—to share with the destitute. Justice was not to have more than that required by our daily needs—"Give us this day our daily bread"—and yet, at the same time, it was to enjoy all the good things God has made.

In seeking a just society, to live as poor among the poor, we cannot live a life of destitution—the destitute poor have no respect for this themselves. They are trying to move upwards, at least to a level of sufficiency for their own needs.

Paul describes a balanced personal justice: "There is great gain in godliness with contentment; for we brought nothing into the world, and we cannot take anything out of the world; but if we have food and clothing, with these we shall be content" (1 Timothy 6:6–8).

Other rich men like St. Francis of Assisi, for the salvation of their own souls, have decided to follow another command—one Jesus gives to the rich young ruler: "If you would be perfect, go, sell what you possess and give to the poor, and you will have treasure in heaven; and come, follow me" (Matthew 19:21).

My observation is that most converted rich are encouraged to do as Abraham and Job—remain rich, but use their wealth wisely, turn their income into capital which can create work for the poor, and live simply yet not be destitute. Unfortunately, despite the number of testimonies we hear from the wealthy and the popularity of "prosperity theology," it is extremely difficult to hang on to our wealth and on to Jesus at the same time. In the house church movement among the rich of Djakarta, Indonesia, believers sagely use the phrase, "Repent of your sins, then repent of your wealth!"

Prosperity theology teaches a "be saved and get rich" Christianity, using the teaching of the Pentateuch, Job and Proverbs about the righteous rich, but ignoring the Psalms, prophets, and teaching of Jesus about the godly poor. Prosperity theology works against genuine spirituality.

Commitment without identification

People often ask, "Were you called to minister to the poor?" We are all called to minister to the poor. Such a ministry is the logical obedience of any disciple imitating the attitudes, character, and teaching of Jesus. He commands everyone to renounce all (Luke 14:33), give to the poor, and live simply. But we would need a special call to minister primarily to the rich or middle-class, for the focus of Christian ministry is "good news to the poor."

Not all, however, are called to a life of *identification* with the poor by living among them!

Is there a reasonable lifestyle for middle-class Filipinos who desire to minister to the poor?

Lazarus, Mary, and Martha are examples of the middle-class of Israel. They had a large home, kept it, and used it for the Lord and his disciples as a retreat center.

I have not discerned God calling many of my middle-class friends to lives of identification with the poor. Some heard and refused his call, but in general, the Lord seemed to be calling them to a ministry among their middle-class peers. To expect them to choose identification with the poor was to expect them to become apostles and missionaries across a great social, economic, and cultural barrier.

Just as the expatriate missionary community is trapped by structures, expectations, and affluence into middle- and upper-class ministries, so the average middle-class Filipino is driven by materialism and the intense demands of upward mobility (through education and post-graduate degrees). Many of the *nouveau riche* in the Philippines come from genuine poverty. They are compelled by family responsibilities to keep moving up to take their family safely out of the danger of poverty. The poor who are still poor constitute a danger to this class. Any relationship to poor people outside of their own clan would drain hard-won finances.

To expect people from this class to jump the class barrier and live among the poor was expecting more than I myself had sacrificed. Never having experienced *involuntary* poverty it was much easier for me, as a "rich Westerner" and a member of the "upper class," to choose *voluntary* poverty. I still had resources, security and friends. But for a person waging personal and family warfare with poverty, there is no romance in returning to a life of frugality.

Nevertheless, like Lazarus, Mary, and Martha, the middle-class can have a significant commitment to the poor. Some fifteen of these middle-class co-laborers have spent extensive time helping in the slums, some making attempts to help economically, some with a Bible study group with a poor family. Others come and stay overnight, some for two or three weeks, to provide companionship.

I couldn't call such people to live among the poor. The best I could do was to set the pace, trusting God to inspire some others by my example. And I could speak of Jesus who tells us: "As thou didst send me into the world, so I have sent them into the world" (John 17:18).

The Carpenter's justice

He had been born as a little babe in a dairy shed; he grew up as a refugee child. His parents were so poor, they could not afford a sheep at his dedication and so had to offer two turtledoves. Tradition tells us that as a teenager he worked to support his mother and family. He chose to be a rabbi, men renowned for their poverty, rather than a rich high priest. He had no place to lay his head. He had calloused hands, wore wooden sandals, and died a poor man's death.

He was Jesus, the just one! Nobody could fault him for economic injustice in his standard of living. Justice demanded equality between the sent one and people. Justice demanded identification or "solidarity" with the poor. He lived at the level of the people, identifying himself with them in voluntary simplicity.

Jesus, the just one, asked more from his middle-class companions than acceptance of the status quo. He demanded renunciation of possessions: "So therefore, whoever of you does not renounce all that he has cannot be my disciple" (Luke 14:33).

He told his team: "Fear not, little flock . . . Sell your possessions, and give alms; provide yourself with purses that do not grow old, with a treasure in the heavens that does not fail" (Luke 12:32–33).

Jesus here used the word "forsake" or "renounce." It is an action word; it is not just an attitude.

Many of us would like it to focus purely on attitude: "Whoever has many possessions, but uses them wisely will be my disciple." But Jesus was very blunt. It is junk *or* Jesus. Just junk or just Jesus—not junk *and* Jesus. Forsake first an attitude, but let the attitude result in action.

You cannot serve God and affluence, says Jesus elsewhere (Matthew 6:24). Not "may not," but *cannot!* There is no choice.

But what does Jesus mean by renouncing *all?* Our Lord did not live in destitution. He grew up in a good home, possessed carpenter's tools, probably played with toys as a child and had a common purse (bank account) with the disciples. He wore clothes. He had breakfast each morning.

He was not a beggar; he was not unemployed. He provided for his twelve followers through the ministry of women (Luke 8:3). They always had enough. He told them (in Matthew 6) that the Father would provide their food and clothing.

"Food and clothing" is a phrase for basic necessities. It may include shelter, work tools, books, children's toys, decorations, and provision for celebration. In most situations today, it involves buying a home—just as the Levites were to own no possessions in Israel, but were to have their own home and enough garden to provide for themselves. But the same phrase excludes a life of ease, luxury, and wealth. It is not a call to destitute poverty, but it *is* a call to simplicity. Just as involuntary and destitute poverty has no intrinsic virtue, so wealth often destroys spirituality.

The attitudes involved are important. But at issue is whether we will eliminate external, glittering possessions and follow him, developing an internal concentration on him—unfettered and unhindered by excess material baggage.

One way to apply this, a symbolic start, is to sit down with our families and go through each of our possessions and the use of our money to get rid of all excess—whatever detracts in time, money, and energy from Christ.

Celebration!

But Jesus was no ascetic. He came eating, drinking, and enjoying life, and was much criticized by the "Bible-believers" of his day for his lack of frugality.

Job, too, enjoyed feasting and drinking. The Old Testament is full of commands for festivals and celebration. We need to live out a "celebrating lifestyle of renunciation."

Ironically, the conflict between the biblical concepts of celebration and renunciation was resolved in my mind one day as I was sitting relaxing with some middle-class friends eating ice cream. The Lord brought to mind the passage immediately preceding his call to renunciation: "When you give a dinner or a banquet, do not invite your . . . rich neighbors . . . But when you give a feast, invite the poor, the maimed, the lame, the blind, and you will be blessed, because they cannot repay you" (Luke 14:12–14).

We are to enjoy life, but *with* and *for* the poor and needy. We are to die to our economic selves, but we are to live glorious economic resurrection lives for others.

My message to the middle-class could be summed up by the following five slogans:

Earn much
Consume little
Hoard nothing
Give generously
Celebrate life.

Chapter Seven

Point of Attack

DISCERNING A MINISTRY STRATEGY

We knew of no missionaries who had chosen to work among the squatters and plant churches. I began searching among aid agencies for patterns or models of ministry. I looked also at the lives of people of God in history who had walked the path of poverty.

A friend had studied the work of the Salvation Army. We enthusiastically discussed General Booth's original scheme for reaching London in the 1890's and its applicability to Manila in the 1980's.[1] I laughed at the difference between Booth and myself. He was tough. He came from among the poor. He was an evangelist. I am not tough, and I find it hard to live among the poor, let alone to minister effectively to them.

As a result of this discussion, I visited the leader of the Salvation Army Social Services. He was a sandy-haired Englishman dressed in the century-ancient Salvation Army uniform. He was flanked by beautiful, smiling Filipino faces, all in similar English-style uniforms. Such is the amazing Filipino adaptability and capacity to integrate other cultures!

Apart from certain cultural anachronisms, I was deeply impressed by their work in the slums. It was small but effective, combining vocational training with Christian ministry.

A year later I had an hour with this man of God when a bus I was on broke down. I boarded the next bus, saw his familiar white face, and squeezed into a neighboring seat. As I listened to his story, I learned about saving people's souls and transforming their environment.

Kagawa of Japan

But my biggest encouragement was the life of another who had suffered no encouragement at first: Kagawa of Japan. His life gave me a realistic model of how to integrate evangelism with the fight against poverty.

Over the years, my hall of fame has grown to include the lives of Calvin, Finney, Booth, Wesley, Assisi, Xavier, Mother Teresa, and many others committed to the poor.

There are marked differences in the lives of these people. Yet all understood the centrality of preaching. And all understood the necessity of focusing on the poor as a priority.

Kagawa, Assisi, and Xavier lived as poor men among the poor. Booth, Wesley, and Calvin chose simple lifestyles. All moved from lives as pure evangelists to become evangelistic social reformers: fighters against sin and fighters against poverty and social injustice at every level of society.

Kagawa began with a commitment to identification, choosing to live in the slums of Shinkawa. But he soon realized that a "spiritual" approach of preaching and teaching alone was insufficient. Those early years, however, were full of the essential experiences of identification. Through the positive response to his work in these years, the next phase of his work was founded.

From pure evangelism, he started a small dispensary and distributed food to beggars. During a time of study in the United States, he realized that he must work at the level of social reform if he was to rescue these slum people.

He had been so busy working among the slum people that he had not thought about dealing with the problem of the slums themselves.

When he returned to Shinkawa, he saw that, although much had been done, many of the things for which he had labored so hard had been lost. The mission was continuing, but without his personal active interference on the side of righteousness, young people had failed to withstand the forces of evil. Three of the girls had been sold as prostitutes, and forty of the boys were in prison for theft and other crimes. These things deepened his convictions that the problem of poverty itself would have to be tackled.

Where people were undernourished and their hours of work long, tuberculosis spread. Kagawa knew that work hours had to be shortened by legislation. Prostitution was a consequence of poverty. Poverty must be dealt with if he would save young believers from returning to this lifestyle. Drink was an escape mechanism. Exploited workers needed reformed legislation.

"We must get rid of poverty . . . force the Government to acknowledge the workers' rights to form unions . . . sweep away the slums," he preached.

There was embarrassment, anger, and hostility. Talk about political action or economic schemes and the reply was always the same: "It isn't the job of the church."

Kagawa saw that his future was bound up with three demands: 1) He must show that Christianity was not remote from the joyful yet dirty business of daily living which could only be demonstrated by continuing to live in the limiting, sordid environment of Shinkawa; 2) Besides demonstrating practical compassion, he must go out in the name of Christ and try to find some solution to the labor problem of Japan; and 3) In doing so, he would alienate many of his fellow Christians and expose himself to official wrath.

From this point, he rapidly became involved in the establishing of trade unions—at a time when they were yet illegal and strikes were still illegal. The power of his leadership was seen in his ability to control strikes with his preaching as much as his readiness to speak in favor of them. His preaching of non-violence enabled the movement to remain out of the hands of the communists at critical points. It was this that finally permitted peaceful negotiations for the existence of trade unions in Japan.

Kagawa, in speaking to laborers, left no doubt of his own position. "Unions are necessary," he said. "But labor problems can only be solved by a change in the heart of the laborer himself."

Kagawa went on to deal with the cause of urban poverty—rural poverty—and many other major social and political projects. But never did he lose his primary cutting-edge as a preacher of the cross of Christ. He eventually stood before the Emperor of Japan to preach the gospel.

Assisi, the great 13th century evangelist to the poor and disciplemaker of the rich, was also a wandering evangelist. He, too, was a social reformer, whose preaching led to economic repentance. At one time in his own strife-torn city of Assisi he acted as arbiter between the two factions that rent its peace: the rich, the *majores,* who were in conflict with the poor, the *minores.*

The document drawn up between them compelled the rich to consult the poor in making agreements with other cities. The lords, in consideration of a small, periodical payment were to renounce all the feudal rights; the inhabitants of the villages surrounding Assisi were to be put on a par with those of the city. Foreigners were protected, the assessment of taxes was fixed, and the exiled poor were allowed to return.[2]

Save souls . . . save bodies . . . save society

"Do we save men's souls or save their environment?" How often have I heard this question—a question that shouldn't even be asked? Theologians put it in more abstruse terms: "Do we work for the transformation of the individual or the transformation of the structures of society?"

These questions come from the Greek separation of mankind into spirit and body. The Hebrew people, who shared Jesus' concept of life, knew no such dichotomy.

As if Kagawa had a choice! He began changing individuals. He soon recognized he must change individuals *and* the environment that holds us in our bondage.

Did I have a choice between saving souls and saving bodies when a vacant lot beside my friend's house was covered with rat-infested garbage? The politicians had called a meeting, discussed the need, and even had a garbage pit dug, but still the field of garbage grew. I asked the Christians to bring shovels. For a whole morning we shoveled the putrid rotting food, the rusty cans, the small snakes, cockroaches, ants, and poisonous centipedes into the hole and set it alight.

A lady approached from a neighboring house, "O praise God!" she said. "Last night I prayed, 'Lord, I am unable alone to shift this rubbish.' But day after day, the winds blow its disease into my small house. Now, here you are, an answer to prayer."

I smiled and told her, "Yes, God is so gracious, isn't he? He wants us not only to be free from the rubbish of the sin in our hearts, so we can be saved; he also wants us to be free from the rubbish in our environment, so we can *live! He* wants us to be rulers over our creation!"

Still the trucks promised by the politicians did not arrive. These squatters had no bribe money; rich businesses did. The garbage filled the field again.

One prayer meeting night with other young squatter believers, I felt constrained to pray that God would completely get rid of this rubbish beside my friend's house.

The next day, workers came. They got rid of the garbage and posted a large sign: "It is forbidden to throw rubbish here: fine P100. Signed: Barrio Captain."

We are called to save souls. We are called to save the bodies of the children who get sick through the disease of a garbage dump. There is no choice between souls and environment.

The primacy of proclamation

While avoiding the traditional errors of our evangelical heritage in "spiritualizing" the kingdom of God, a commitment to the Scriptures needs, on the other hand, to beware of the other end of the pendulum. The final aim of mission is not socio-economic-political change.

One day, I curled up in a soft chair in the magnificent Manila Peninsula Hotel. (At times I would take a whole day off to get some peace and quiet, and again experience air-conditioning and Western culture. Everybody assumed I was a tourist. God gives us all good things to enjoy!) This day I read right through the Gospel of Mark to see if there was any way I could accommodate the teaching that the aim of mission is socio-economic-political change.

There was no way. The Gospels are clear. The establishment of the kingdom is accomplished not primarily by political change, economic change, or social change. It is accomplished by people preaching the good news that the kingdom of God has come. The kingdom comes as people repent of their sins against God, of their economic exploitation and their social hatreds, and submit themselves to the teaching of the King. Demonstrations of spiritual power, seen in spiritual gifts of healing and power over demons, accompany this proclamation.

As a result of proclamation, new communities of believers form within towns and cities. These communities often will be persecuted, and politically will not be powerful. But they are to act as salt does in meat and be a sign of righteousness.

Unmet needs

I began to ask questions and discovered that official and unofficial estimates of the squatter and slum population range from 1.8 million to 3.6 million—30–40 percent of Manila's population, growing at a rate of 12 percent per year.

We found ten evangelical aid programs among these millions. A number of churches also had extension Bible studies into the slums. A few local Catholic priests lived with the poor. But of the more than 400 missionaries living in Manila, not one was actually living among the poor.

After eight years of searching, we found just six Filipino pastors who have lived in these slums and established significant churches. That is one church for every 500,000 squatters— equivalent to one church for the entire state of Alaska. What further reason is needed for a life of proclamation and identification with the squatters of the slums of Asia?

Most Christian agencies to the poor had been captured by the social work concept: the basic issues are the economic issues; the entrance point is economic programs. One should only attach an evangelist to such programs and have Bible studies for the recipients of the aid after the economic need has been met.

This error of many evangelical aid agencies appears to be not so much theological as tactical. The entrance point into communities in the Scripture *is not* aid programs, projects, or good deeds. It is the breaking down of demonic powers by the proclamation of the cross. This is accomplished in the context of doing good deeds and results in spiritual change, which in turn transforms social, economic, and cultural values.

Because of their deep commitment to the proclamation of the gospel, the Salvation Army has a fine balance between the social and spiritual in their work. They see their social work as a pastoral component of ministry and only begin after the establishment of a local "corps," usually a year later. Even in community projects among the people, their workers always see Christian salvation as the priority. Their vibrant passion for seeing people turn to God is balanced with the expectation of economic transformation following spiritual transformation.

Any disciple with a burning sense of mission must proclaim the kingdom. Economic programs may be added in any number of ways to such a person's work, but the power of proclamation is the essential starting point for any growth of the kingdom.

There is no question of spiritual versus material. The kingdom is holistic. But a definite set of priorities brings about socio-economic-spiritual change in a community:

1. Proclamation leads to disciplemaking.

2. Disciplemaking leads to pastoral issues.

3. Pastoral issues result in building a new social structure where economic needs can be discussed and enumerated.

4. A new social structure involves dealing with politicians and seeking changes in public policy or political personnel.

What about social work?

Social work and community development are, indeed, significant areas of Christian activity to the extent that they are reflections of biblical teaching on social relationships, financial dealing, and political action. Workers for the kingdom of God can work with government and private agencies working in the squatter areas.

At the same time the kingdom comes violently (but not by violence!), so that its truth may at times create disharmony. People persecute Christians for living and preaching the truth (John 15:18–25), which according to their standards, is a violation of professional humanistic social work ethics.

Social situations

Having determined the primacy of proclamation, we still need to discern how and when to grapple with broken social structures, inadequate economic opportunities, and corrupt political structures. The following list in Manila shows some of the possible points of attack:

CLASSES OF URBAN POOR

- Squatter areas (approx. 2 million)
- Slum areas (approx. 1 million)
- Families in other parts of the city living below the marginal level
- Disabled and handicapped
- Youth offenders, unemployed youth, drug addicts
- Unemployed and under-employed, laborers
- Exploited factory workers
- Orphans and widows, prostitutes

Which need?

The following is a brief review of some of the problems of the urban poor.

1. Demonic influences of an animistic/Catholic culture

The continued heritage of animism, the appeasing of saints, spirits, and even God himself, is in direct contradiction with the biblical view of humanity as the ruler of God's creation.

Perceiving success as the blessing of the spiritual powers (or added graces from God) leads to a *bahala na* ("it's up to fate or God or spirits") attitude that precludes pre-planning, management skills, and commitment to work with the hands.

Worship of saints, use of curses, prayers to the dead, and other practices often are related to sickness and emotional disturbances.

POINTS OF ATTACK IN THE FIGHT AGAINST POVERTY

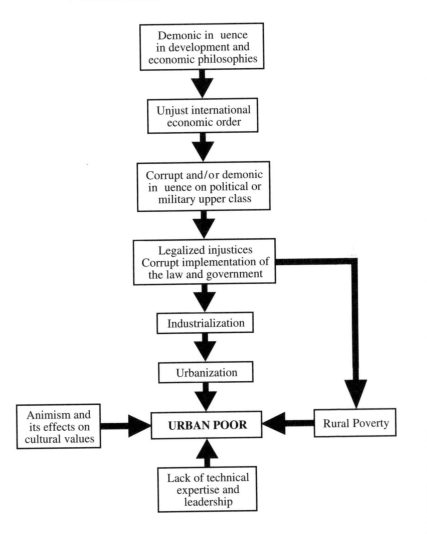

2. Unemployment

Basic to the meeting of most needs is the need for income. A survey of 1,500 adults over fifteen years of age in one established slum in Manila showed that 1,191 of them, or 68 percent, were unemployed.[3] The remaining 32 percent were employed in the following occupations:

OCCUPATIONS OF ADULTS IN ONE MANILA SLUM

Bar girls (hostesses)	105	Shoe repairmen	6
Unskilled laborers	102	Salesmen	6
Vendors	55	Gov't employees	5
Drivers	89	Hospital attendants	5
Dressmakers	40	Storekeepers	5
Waitresses/Waiters	30	Masseurs	5
Scavengers	12	Hairdressers	4
Manicurists	10	Stable boys	4
Laundry women	10	Electricians	4
Gasoline boys	10	Janitors	3
Bouncers	10	Midwives	3
Barbers	10	Mechanics	3
Bus conductors	10	Bakers	3
Tailors	9	Policemen	2
Carpenters	7	Butchers	1

Notice in the above industrial context, the number of tradesmen consists of seven carpenters, four electricians and three mechanics—a total of 14 workmen out of 568, or a mere 2.5 percent (assuming that all the above were in fact skilled). The statistics reveal one of the slum's critical needs: the introduction of practical trade skills.

3. Inadequate housing

Filipinos call them "squatters," which aptly describes the insecurity of the new city migrant. Too poor to purchase land and build a house within a reasonable time, unwilling to pay rent for decaying accommodation or perhaps unable to find a room for his family, the migrant is forced to illegally occupy land. He becomes a squatter on land in dispute, unused public land or buildings, frequently flooded land, or land beside railway tracks.

Two-Thirds World communities have neither the money nor the technical skills to mount a housing program on the scale demanded by recent immigration to the cities. Four approaches have been tried:

(a) providing unaffordable housing estates,

(b) eliminating or ejecting squatters *en masse* from land,

(c) providing sites and infrastructure, enabling the site owner to construct his own house, and

(d) upgrading existing areas over a period of time.

The third and fourth options provide some hope, but in most mega-cities, the absence of an effective comprehensive policy for housing the poor reflects a preference in allocating scarce resources for the richer classes. This problem has no easy solutions. Solutions that worked in nineteenth century Europe are no longer applicable. The problem of housing will grow, and we must do all we can to alleviate it.

4. Unsanitary environment

The fact that squatter housing is illegal means that garbage collection, sewerage, water supply, and electricity have to be obtained illegally or informally. Unsanitary conditions cause frequent sickness. Malnutrition further adds to the sickness and death toll.

5. Lack of education

Whether or not education is available, families cannot afford to send their children to school. Working, as opposed to school, meets a more immediate need—money. Lack of elementary education destroys any future of higher education or better employment.

6. Broken social structure

The uprooting of millions from their provincial roots into an environment lacking traditional social controls leads to an almost total breakdown of moral values, community, and family relationships. Immorality, gambling, and drunkenness run unchecked. Gang warfare is frequent.

7. Destitutes

These areas also become the final dwelling place for the failures, outcasts, and dropouts of society. For widows, orphans, deaf, dumb, blind, alcoholic, drug-addicted, and all classes of unfortunates, the slum is the only place to live.

8. Injustice, oppression, exploitation

Prostitution and slavery are common means of exploitation. But even those who have legal work are exploited. Corrupt politicians, landowners, businessmen, and others cheat the people and create deeper poverty.

9. The future

This trend towards urbanization may slow down. However, the immediate future shows no evidence of any solutions. The problems will grow for some time.[4]

Proposed measures of rural development are not likely to stem emigration from the provinces to the cities. The prevailing patterns of economic dependence of the Two-Thirds World nations on the industrial nations will perpetuate and increase the social inequalities within poor nations. Radical structural reforms may be difficult to bring to completion due to the status of dependency on the developed world. The very scale of the problem is beyond what most governments can cope with. Efforts are likely to be concentrated in a few areas to the neglect of the remainder.

The slum and squatter communities themselves will slowly change. Immigrants will be better educated than those of former decades, and the proportion of second-generation squatters will increase.

The state and para-state bureaucracy will not be able to create jobs for more than a minority of migrants and primary school dropouts. Most will have to be absorbed into the informal sector—into small-scale labor-intensive activity, poverty, and patronage, dependent on the formal sector, working long hours for low financial return.

Mobility through education is likely to be slight, as is the chance of upward mobility in the entrepreneurial sector.

Yet the people will continue to hope. The story of the local boy who has "made good" will have more influence than statistics indicating the improbability of success.

NOTES

1. General William Booth, *In Darkest England and the Way Out* (Amazon Press, 2001).

2. Paul Sabatier, *The Road To Assisi: The Essential Biography Of St. Francis,* Jon Sweeney, ed., (Paraclete Press, 2004).

3. Landa F. Jocano, *Slums as a Way of Life* (Quezon City: University of the Philippines Press, 1975), 31.

4. These thoughts are summarized from Peter Lloyd, *Slums of Hope Shanty Towns of the Third World* (Pelican Books, 1979), chapter 9. Reprinted by permission of Penguin Books Ltd. More recent comprehensive research on the nature of the slums, is available in UN-Habitat, *The Challenge of the Slums: Global Report on Human Settlements* (Earthscan Publications, 2003).

Chapter Eight

New Ministry, New Power
THE REALITY OF GOD IN THE SLUMS

The time had come. We had reflected on and analyzed the causes and issues of squatter poverty. We had developed a theological basis for mission to the poor. The Lord had given us a strategy. But where in Manila, among all of the slums and squatter settlements, should we start?

Choosing a community

For some months before moving to Tatalon, whenever I had free time, I leaped on a motorcycle and roved from squatter community to squatter community.

One day, I rode down the narrow paved road between the old higgledy-piggledy houses of Santa Ana. Down the *kalyes* I could see acre upon acre of galvanized iron and plywood shacks, with one leaning against another. The children here were silent. No "Hi Joe's" as in other places.

Spiritual darkness like the darkened color of the old houses filled the streets. An iconed chapel on the corner avenue loomed over the community. Every house seemed full of images of saints. Other chapels surrounded the community. In the middle of the squalor, a magnificent religious school stood complacently. Symbols of a superficial folk religion dominated the narrow streets and tiny homes. The sense of the demonic was everywhere.

Finally, as I stopped by some older men, I heard the traditional greeting.

"Hey, Joe, where have you come from?"

"I'm lost," I replied. "I see you're having a fiesta soon." I pointed to their decorations across the small main street. They described in detail the celebration to their saint and the Virgin.

Santa Ana—a demonic squatter community. This was not the place to begin the work of God.

The next day, I wandered along a dirt road by a river. Many squatters live on the rivers, where older *barrios* (small villages) existed as a nucleus for poor people to congregate. The rich do not use properties that flood.

The community was surrounded by mile upon mile of heavy industry. Children laughed at me as I passed. Their "Hi, Joe" was one of hatred and derision, not the wide-eyed, smiling banter of usual Filipino hospitality.

The men's faces were sullen and nasty. I could hear the noise of families fighting as I walked through the slum. I quickly turned back from one street after glimpsing the flash of knives drawn between two men.

A fit harvest

And then there were other areas. Among them was Tatalon. As I entered it, I saw people busy building. Laughter filled the backstreets. Children gave me happy smiles. Everywhere, there was activity and a spirit of hope. The Holy Spirit let me know, in his voiceless Spirit-to-spirit communication, that this place was one where he was at work.

Part of the reason for hope was the excellent upgrading program in this community. I have noticed that where economic progress is being made, people are more responsive to the gospel. Positive changes in one area of people's lives gives them a desire for further positive changes.

I spent some time wandering around the streets. A local leader in one area was loading scrap metal into his jeep. "It's hard work that counts," he said. *"Tiyaga, sipa!"* (Patience, industriousness!)

In one area of Tatalon, the upgrading program of the National Housing Authority was well advanced. People worked together to build houses of concrete blocks. The sounds of hammer and saw and the bustle of an active people were evident.

The leader told me of a Catholic priest who had formerly lived there. I walked through the scrambled labyrinth of walls, picking my way across the mud and dirty water trickling along the lane, asking people directions to the home where the priest had lived.

The family with whom he had lived was courteous. This priest had truly lived simply—he was a man given to prayer. But the military had come and deported him. He had been involved in "activism" against the government, fighting against the housing program, and offending the barangay leaders appointed by the Marcos government to lead Tatalon.

He had built a small chapel in which to say mass, but the National Housing Authority had pushed it down because it was illegal. He had become angry.

I visited another priest—a friend and co-worker of the priest who had worked in Tatalon. He was a big, bearded, soft-spoken American. He told me the background of their work in the slum more fully.

Their objective had been to build a basic Christian community. They tried to do it by fighting for justice in the area of housing and then by developing an education program. Both attempts failed. I sensed his frustration as he described the time when the barrio captain had stood by and watched as the Priest was taken to prison for his work as community organizer.

"Do you know of any righteous people, any godly contacts in Tatalon?" I asked.

He said he did not and advised me to live in another section of the community instead of the section where they had struggled. Perhaps there would be more success in another area of the slum.

I let people know I was interested in Tatalon. Georgina, one of thirteen social workers in a National Housing Authority Bible study group, volunteered to take me into the community. She introduced me to the community leaders. We told them of my desire for a home from which to minister spiritually to the people. Three weeks later I was busy cooking in Aling Nena's upper room.

At home at last

As I cooked my rice and fish on the little gas burner and boiled my water, I thought about how to incarnate Christ in this community.

If I was to be the incarnate body of Christ in Tatalon, I must not only dwell there, but let the character of Christ reveal itself in me. I must love. I must give of myself.

However, I alone could not incarnate God. I am but a part of his body. In Filipino culture, a high premium is placed on companionship. For many months I had been asking and praying for someone to join me in this work. Those I asked were all gracious in their refusals. Some had family obligations; some were too busy grappling with their own struggles or their own inadequacies; some were making money; others were earning degrees. Many had not yet fully considered the Word of God about the poor.

Again, the Lord spoke from Luke 14: "But they all alike began to make excuses. The first said to him, 'I have bought a field, and I must go out and see it; I pray you, have me excused.' And another said, 'I have bought five yoke of oxen, and I go to examine them; I pray you, have me excused.' And another said, 'I have married a wife, and therefore I cannot come'" (Luke 14:18–20).

He was telling me to press on regardless of companionship. He would bring some of the poor to provide this: "Go out quickly to the streets and lanes of the city and bring in the poor and maimed and blind and lame. . . . For I tell you none of those men who were invited shall taste my banquet" (Luke 14:21, 24).

And my friends did not desert me. That evening two of my former team members came to help me clean my house. Outside, lightning flashed and thunder roared. We draped plastic over some of the holes in the walls to keep out the tropical rain that pummeled furiously on the roof. I had rescued the cardboard that had come with a friend's fridge, and we used this to line another wall.

The average kill per day was ten cockroaches in this house. (A neighbor killed ninety-eight one day—her children counted them! She used up a whole bottle of my insect spray!) I hung sacks around the inside of the windows to keep the rain out between the cracks. We were careful not to disturb the lizards that lived there. They fed on mosquitoes and other insects. They were friends.

That evening, sitting in my window, I thanked God for providing a center and a home for reaching Manila's poor. My evening prayer was, "Lord, I need a comfort room (toilet) so I don't have to share with twelve others. Otherwise I will get sick."

The next morning, I was scrubbing on my knees with a bucket of water. I heard a shout, "Viv! Viv!" from down the three-step ladder (each step being eighteen inches high) that served as a staircase to my "mansion."

Lisa, the little seven-year-old from below, came up the stairs to my room. *"Si Aling Aging"* (It's Mrs Aging), she said, smiling shyly at me.

I poked my head out the hole above these steps. It was the beaming face of Aling Aging, the barrio councilor. I climbed down into the mid-morning sunshine.

"Would you like to use our extra comfort room?" she inquired, after greeting me with her normal bouncing laugh. (Her husband was a seaman, which is the top economic bracket among squatters. They earn dollars!)

"Is there a spare one?" I asked.

"Yes," she answered. "We have one we don't use. We dug our own at the house."

"I was praying for this very thing last night," I told her happily.

"Come over and get the key from Boy," she said, moving on to visit other houses in the cluster. "We want you to feel at home. We can't afford for you to get sick."

I nodded again, trying to catch the poetry of the Tagalog words. As I finished cleaning, I thought, *It's really quite logical to walk in the steps of the laboring Carpenter.* A song kept running through my mind: "Love was when God became man/Left his timeless place/Dwelt in time and space."

God's incarnation is wrapped in compassion. He saw the unmet needs in the midst of his people and so came.

Reminded of carpenters, I walked across the dusty area outside our house, across the road, past the fourteen toilets all in a row into a carpentry shop that made cheap furniture for squatters. I met the owner and bought some plywood and nails. Two children helped carry it back, and I began to put a ceiling under the smoke blackened and unbearably hot iron roof of my new home.

Fit for a king

How do you describe a squatter home? Ours was built after the model of provincial houses, with good solid corner posts. Over the next few months the floor sagged in the middle a good four or five inches, but it was generally well built.

Nerio came up the stairs to help me finish the roof. He was an expert carpenter and lived downstairs in another quarter of the house with his second wife. After working on the roof, we sat down and had a soda together. He told me about himself—a man skilled yet impoverished by broken family relationships. As we talked, my mind was constantly concentrating on the Tagalog words.

Once, I had been sitting downstairs in Nerio's home and saw a rat running around the room where they slept. I threw a hammer and hit it mid-ribs. It leapt five or six times straight up in the air about two feet and then struggled into a hole. The people didn't comment. Later I discovered that it is wise not to attack rats because they come back and attack you.

Rats kept me awake in my own room the first night, so I bought a rat trap. We caught three of them the next day. But rats also provided entertainment. One night in the kitchen where I had put up the ceiling, I heard the rats start at the top and then zoom all the way down to the bottom of the sloping ceiling. They chuckled and chattered to themselves, climbing back to the top to zoom down again.

I put garbage outside in a little can that was hung from the house in a place where the rats couldn't get it. Old papers were given to Aling Nena. She used them in her little store to wrap her customers' purchases.

The kitchen timbers were old and blackened with the smoke of charcoal fires over the years. The bench was made of a basin and bits of old wood. I used a two-burner gas stove running from a liquid petroleum gas tank. It was much more efficient than the charcoal or kerosene that most squatters use. Because of the cracks in the walls, I could look out to see what was happening at all times from my kitchen.

The squatter area has electricity—most squatters tap the electricity off the power lines. Each night we usually went to the pump to fetch a couple of buckets of water. Our next-door-neighbor washed my clothes for a few pesos each week.

I asked Nerio to make a decent table for the kitchen. He did it in a half day. This was where I would leave my typewriter. Coring, a woman who lived next door, came to type for me two or three days a week. I was able to find her a job typing for another missionary for the other two or three days per week. She had just graduated from a two-year typing course. The kitchen also became a little office.

Windows were vacant holes in the wall that I covered with a piece of wood when it rained. This makeshift "shutter" swung on its hinges like a window at other times. I put the desk borrowed from a missionary friend in the six-by-ten foot bedroom. Like the others, I slept with one sheet on a mat under a mosquito net, rolling up the mosquito net each morning.

It is a strange thing becoming poor among the poor. First, you seek to live at their level—to do exactly what they are doing—and then, as you do that, you recognize and identify those physical or emotional needs you can't live without even though they do.

You make small adjustments. This is acceptable to the people. Identification is not imitation. For example, I needed a good cassette tape recorder for language study. Most folk only had a radio. I also needed a bookcase.

Houses built for an incoming family would be about six-by-ten feet and made of plywood with iron roofing. Older people in the community had put up larger houses which were equivalent to four of these small houses: two rooms upstairs and two rooms downstairs. Four families could live in such a house.

The attractive corner house in our cluster of houses was constructed by a man who had become quite successful in engineering. The lower story had a concrete floor!

Often squatters live beside the railway tracks where there is some vacant land. Roofs are covered with old tires to hold the metal sheet on.

The best homes are raised off the ground, keeping them from the water and giving a little bit of privacy. Soon the bottom of the house is built and new squatters move into that. Often they have relatives. Trees disappear quickly for firewood. Any vacant land nearby is very quickly cultivated to provide vegetables, since many of the squatters are from the province and still have agricultural skills.

Perhaps one home in ten has a television set. Such families may have someone working in an office job who could afford a television. Everybody else watches the television through the windows. It is an appliance that has to be shared.

Possessions are shared among the squatters, but one never enters another's home for a meal or during mealtime. One talks outside, lest the family be embarrassed and forced into buying extra food which they cannot afford for the guest.

Where do the wood and the timber come for building the homes? Sometimes it is from plywood packing cases. Sometimes it is bought. For example, one day Aling Nena came back excited. She'd been out visiting a friend and had seen an old, broken down truck. She had bought the roof off the truck! This would make a good roof for the new *sari-sari* store she wanted to put up.

Life in the slum is a daily pattern. Early in the morning, teenage girls use their straw brooms to sweep the dust off the bare earth between houses. Mothers sit on their haunches washing in their basins, or washing and soaping their hair. Others, dressed beautifully, head off to work, walking between the plywood homes under the washing, dodging the puddles, laughing and talking with friends. Radios blare to waken the neighbors who have managed to sleep through the cacophony of shouting mothers and children.

The middle of the day is a time to stay out of the sun. Usually there is a *siesta*. Around three o'clock is the time for gambling. Women have little to do at this time, and it becomes a good time for women's activities.

Then, while the women cook the rice, everyone sits outside their houses to talk over the day's events as the sun sets. This is the time for friendship and evangelism.

God-sent overcoat

One thing was clear. Before I could effectively preach the gospel to the poor, I must know deeply the power of God. Before Jesus began his ministry, the Spirit "descended on him in bodily form, as a dove" and he became "full of the Holy Spirit" (Luke 3:22; 4:1).

I wanted to know that power of God. In the hunger and search for him, I had scavenged in an infinite number of the cracks and crevices of life. Now at the place of his call, my inner being, so much a desert, still hungered for that inner knowledge of God.

I knew that in obedience comes such knowledge: "He who has my commandments and keeps them, he it is who loves me; and he who loves me will be loved by my Father, and I will love him and manifest myself to him" (John 14:21).

In the Scriptures, it is clear that in powerlessness he displays his power, in poverty he reveals his riches, in the cross he shows his resurrection, and in brokenness he displays his healing power. The Spirit of power is first a Spirit of fire, burning the chaff from our lives, burning out the dross of sin.

As I chose to direct myself in this way of poverty—of brokenness, of powerlessness—God was not slow to respond in revealing himself in his sovereign way.

He began to sensitize my spirit to his with a deep time of intense loneliness. During those early days, loneliness not only walked with me, it hung like an oversized, great coat. It had always been a friend, but now became my ever-present companion.

Friends among the professionals did not visit—some too busy, some afraid to enter the community, but most preferring to avoid the criticism of others who disagreed with any move into the slums. Some of the gossip was quite painful and eventually did much harm; but, since it would have taken days of discussion to track down and deal with its source, I watched it multiply like a cancer and left it up to God's mercy.

Along with the feeling of aloneness, I felt Satan attack wave after wave. Fever lasted several days; I experienced an unpleasant rash; doubt and discouragement sought to overwhelm. The constant failure that is a normal part of any ministry and of culture shock continued.

During those first days in Tatalon, my thoughts could well have echoed Kagawa's simple words:

> I came to bring
> God to the slum;
> But I am dumb
> Dismayed
> Betrayed
> By those
> Whom I would aid;
> Pressed down
> So sad
> I fear
> That I am mad.
> Pictures
> Race through my brain
> And lie
> Upon my heart
> Pictures like this
> A man
> Legs rotted off

> With syphilis
> And yet
> He need not fret
> That money
> Does not come
> Because his wife
> Is rented out
> And brings
> Sufficient sum
> One month in the slums
> And I am sad,
> So sad,
> Seem devil-possessed
> Or mad[1]

Like Kagawa, I would have turned back but for the call of the One who loved me and who commanded: "No one who puts his hand to the plow and looks back is fit for the kingdom of God" (Luke 9:62). "My righteous one shall live by faith, and if he shrinks back, my soul has no pleasure in him" (Hebrews 10:38).

Such verses were often the final motivation I needed to press on into the darkness, the danger, the hatred. I wrote: "No friends, no companion, no ease or comfort, no position or power have I sought, none of these wanted. Yet, the poor are still far from me and so too is my distant God. I must yet go deeper into that cross. Somewhere in the fullness of his suffering, he will meet me."

And God did! As the light fills and illuminates, so his light began to fill and to flood my life in the midst of darkness. Day by day I would spend hours in the Word of God and in prayer. Surrounded by drunkenness, oppression, and immorality, God's love filled and cleansed me in a way I had never before experienced. Renewal and a fullness of the power of God began to radiate out to the destitute around. People I prayed for during that time were the ones who were later converted. God began to reveal his power.

As a child, I had experienced the overwhelming presence of the love of God as it flowed over and over me day after day. Before I lived in Tatalon, there were times when I had seen his anointing on his word as I preached. Throughout my life, I had seen God's spirit descend on people. But in Tatalon, he began to break forth with a new power and joy. I had experienced times when the spiritual gifts that he gave at conversion had been evident, but now there was a deeper sensitivity to him, a freer flow. A cleansing of old sin and traditions unleashed these gifts.

As a youth I had seen a pattern from reading hundreds of the biographies of the great saints. Somewhere, ten to fifteen years into their ministries, they often entered into a deeper life, a new empowering of the Spirit of God. They used various terms, and came from various doctrinal persuasions. Some spoke of "Christ in me." Corrie Ten Boom told of "entering his rest." Others talked of the "immersion of the Spirit," "release in the Spirit," or the "baptism of the Spirit." Others described a continued series of "fillings of the Spirit;" some spoke of the "anointing of God."

A diversity of doctrine on this issue is good, for the wind blows where it wills and we hear the sound of it, but we do not know from where it comes or to where it goes, so it is with the Spirit (John 3:8). God is not an abstract doctrine. He is alive and sovereign. He had met me and now began to move in new ways beyond my prayers and work. For so long, my ministry had been such a struggle, so dependent on *me*. Now I had difficulty keeping up with *him!* But I could see that Satan was not weak in the counter-attack.

In counseling others on the secret of life in the Spirit, I have found no set formula. All I can do is point to the cross—to its suffering, to the obedience it demands, to the discipline it imposes, to the power of its proclamation, to its absolute authority.

Many Christians want power, few want holiness. Many want the resurrected life, few want the cross.[2]

The Spirit world

One of the first evidences of a new power was in confrontations with demons.

In the slums, one comes more and more into direct demonic confrontation. The Lord began to train me in this area, too.

One day I was doing some business in Makati, the rich city in Metro-Manila, when the Spirit of God began to speak to me very strongly. I needed to go home. When that happens, one acts quickly! I hurried home. As I arrived, a leader in the ministry also arrived.

"Your engineer friend, Raul, is calling for you. He is attacked by a demon." We ran quickly to the house.

Some days earlier, Raul heard an evangelist who told him to "listen to the Spirit." He began to listen and initially what he heard was in line with the Scriptures. But as he kept listening, another spirit began to speak, saying, "God is light. The sun is light. Worship the sun."

Raul had thrown away his shoes, his wallet, and his shirt under the instructions of this spirit before the police picked him up.

The family was angry at Raul for having read the Bible and getting involved with a spirit. Finally, because the spirit gave him no sleep, Raul told them, "Bring me over to the ministry center." There, they read the Scriptures and prayed. Raul joined in the prayers, but repeatedly, as the spirit troubled him, he would stop praying.

When I arrived, I didn't know what to do, so I asked questions to find out what had happened. Then I prayed, commanding the spirit to leave. Raul would begin to rest, and then once again the spirit would return—talking, talking, and talking to him. We prayed again.

I asked Naty, his wife, to begin to read the Scriptures. Whenever she did, the evil spirit would depart again. She prayed

Some of the pastoral team and believers celebrating

Henry, George, and their extended family

Wherever land is available, squatters erect their homes—often beside rivers and waterways

Drainage in Tatalon: open and above ground

Good jobs in the market: A revolving loan helped fund this meat stall

Rice cake seller

Paster Jun (2nd from left) and a barkada Bible Study

The daily routine of fetching water from the pump

to become a Christian. We told Raul how to use the name of Christ against the spirit. After more prayer, it left without much of a fight.

His father arrived with a jeep-load of people. Among them was a man with sharp, piercing eyes who kept saying, "You know there is somebody higher than Jesus Christ." I recognized him as a medium. They had brought him to cast the demon from Raul. We explained that prayer, the Scriptures, and the name of Christ had already freed him.

We discussed the event for a long time. Finally, his father was satisfied with our suggestion that in two days' time Raul should return to the province where we would gather the neighbors and explain how he became freed. This would save the family honor.

Two days later, we all boarded a jeep back to the province. Neighbors gathered. Relatives gathered. People stood all around the windows looking in.

Raul gave his testimony. Milleth sang and Pastor Jun preached. We talked until midnight. Many believed that day, and the Lord wrought a great victory indeed, turning the tables on Satan.

My brother, the professor

God used my relationship with another close friend to give me a deeper understanding of how to grapple with the spirit world.

A few months before moving into Tatalon, I received a request from a friend to take over the follow-up of a professor and of a politician he was helping. Both were doing PhDs at the University of the Philippines. I sensed that God was evident in this request.

The professor was the father of eleven children and professor of graduate studies at Isabella State University. He was a big man, a leader, a man of high standing among the Ibanag (Ee-ba-nag) people. His relatives were mayors and city officials. He was also a gifted orator.

About 336,000 Ibanag people live in and around the Cagayan Valley in Northern Luzon. They are a dignified and proud people, with a strong sense of identity and culture. Until now, no significant breakthrough for the gospel has taken place among the Ibanags since the initial thrust of evangelical Methodism in the early 1900s.

After the professor's conversion, God gave him boldness to invite first one, then three to a Bible study group. The principal of the high school came to Christ. Others came.

The professor saw a little sick boy, put his hand on his head and prayed. He was healed. This happened several times. He came back to visit us in Manila. I sat with him and the soft-spoken research assistant who had led him in Bible studies. He shared his experiences and then asked, "Do you think this is from God? Do you think God will take it away?"

We encouraged him, and a month later took a team up to Isabella to run a three-day "Dynamics of Christian Growth" seminar.

When he invited me to preach at his Bible study, seventy people attended. What a work of the Spirit of God! After the seminar, four high-school-aged attendees went back and led one hundred others to Christ—almost their entire school.

But much of the professor's early life had been marred by cruelty. In his relationship to his own family, he had to learn to apply the Scriptures. My role was to be one of friendship and encouragement to build balance, character, and depth in the Word.

Late one night, we sat up with him as he poured out the terrible cruelty and pain and asked the Lord to heal each memory. He began to show love to his children, and God began to fully restore his relationship with his wife and family.

Despite many obstacles, the gospel moved so rapidly that within six months over a thousand Ibanag people had turned to Christ.

As a leader in the community, the professor was frequently invited by his relatives (often the mayors of neighboring towns) to preach in their barrios or in the neighboring chapels. (At this point, the parish priest was positive towards the movement since he himself had translated much of the Scriptures into Ibanag.) When he would preach, it would often last two or three hours. People loved to hear the oratory in their own dialect.

The director of a tobacco research unit invited us to address his thirty workers during office hours. As time passed and the cross was preached, the men began to weep. After the message, the professor said, "Now would all those who have not believed stand up." They all remained seated. Later, the decision would be personalized, but in Ibanag culture, decisions are made in a group context.

Couples were reunited, drunkards released, people healed. In one weekend there were four encounters where demons were cast out.

The army officers of the province asked him to come and speak. He interpreted for them a biblical approach to development in their province, beginning with the gospel and with spiritual and cultural liberation.

Why should God use a two-year-old Christian in such a dynamic way? The history of church growth illustrates that when God wants to break open a tribe held long in animism, he will often choose one of the tribal leaders within the movement. Then he will empower such a person to confront the spirit powers of the tribe.[3]

Missionaries have often failed to exploit such opportunities. Discipling movements must quickly follow behind such a response of people turning to Christ. Fortunately, the leaders within REACH were sensitive to the Lord. We were able to dispatch one of the key ministry leaders to assist the professor in consolidating and building a core team of people who could disciple new believers.

We encouraged him to remain within the Catholic framework. To move out would create a socio-cultural barrier and prevent the full consummation of the movement. But eventually, the public burning of idols created a wide rift, and he came into direct conflict with the Catholic Church in his preaching against idols and worship of saints.

Wisely, his gospel message focused around the difference between the biblical worldview of spirits and the Ibanag worldview. In the Ibanag worldview, good and bad spirits coexist. Good spirits assist people to do good and to heal. Life is spent in appeasing both bad and good spirits. Despite the people becoming Catholic in name, this was still their worldview. The Catholic saints and the Virgin Mary were added to the pantheon of spirits that needed appeasing. The real break with Catholicism is the break with animism. Moreover, this occurs when the idols—the "saints"—are destroyed. That is conversion!

Guerrilla warfare

One situation that had bothered me as I was recruiting the team to come and assist in the slums was the demonic attacks on the family of Manuel.

I had a long talk with his father. He had been a guerrilla fighter during the Second World War and was now head of a technical university. Their family was one of the leading families of the province—a good, God-loving, and important family.

He sat back in his chair and, as is the custom of older Filipino men when entertaining, began to tell us a number of stories. These were about his dealings with the spirits.

First, he told how as an officer in the Engineers during the war, as they were making a road through the mountain province, they came to a row of five trees. The first four trees required only a stick of dynamite to move them. But the fifth, after a single charge, did not move. They used a whole box of dynamite on it next. It still did not move. Finally, they placed three boxes at the foot of the tree. To their amazement, the tree lifted up and flew horizontally to the ground several meters away, taking the boxes along with it.

Later, two men assigned to dig under the tree struck the grave of a mountain king. Within six hours they died. Manuel's father also began to get a deep fever. He called his men to find the local witch doctor. The medium came, prayed for him, and he survived.

At another time in the mountain province, he slept in a hollow, also a burial place of the mountain kings. The people warned them that nobody had ever been able to sleep there. He and his companion could not sleep. A dream returned to him time and again of some men trying to scoop them up in a net. In the morning, he discovered that his companions had had the same dream.

His father was a good man, a devout Catholic leader. He read the Scriptures faithfully. Yet true to the Ibanag worldview, he believed that many of these spirits were good and helpful and could enable him to gain control over evil spirits, and even to heal the sick. I learned that Manuel's aunt was a medium. Catholicism, after four centuries, had been powerless to confront the basic core of animistic beliefs of these people.

I took the professor over one night and the two men swapped stories about their dealings with the spirits. The professor explained the difference between the biblical worldview and the Ibanag worldview (spirits are good but mischievous and need to be appeased).

Manuel's father told us about the time his whole family had been together. A spirit had taken over one of the brothers, and spoken to them of the sins of the family.

We prayed with him, but there was no apparent revelation given to him. Then we went up to Manuel's room and commanded the spirit to leave. Goose pimples ran up my spine. Our hair stood on end. The spirit appeared to have gone at the time, but a year later, the family was still being troubled.

This family will finally be free when, as a family, they completely renounce their dealings with the spirit world.

Warfare of rest

This continuing experience of "Christ being my life," of it being "no longer I, but Christ in me," resulted in more than power in proclamation and in dealing with demons. There has come an ever-growing knowledge of "the rest of Christ." By knowing that the risen Christ is working, we can quietly relax and watch him work—though at the same time we may be all action, too. His rest is a quiet confidence that not only is he working, but that he will bring everything to successful completion.

People ask, "In the midst of so much poverty and suffering, how can you cope with all the needs?"

The answer is, I don't have to. That is God's task!

At times, I used to be so afraid of being in the slum that I would take the jeepney past the squatter community, traveling on for several minutes until I had been able to review some of the passages of the Scripture that gave me promises of God's protection. Psalm 121:7–8 told me: "The LORD will keep you from all evil; The LORD will keep your life. He will keep your going out and your coming in from this time forth and for evermore."

Finally, I would get off the jeepney, take another jeepney back, and walk through the squatter community to my home. The people always seemed to be reaching out to be talked to, to be ministered to, to be loved. I didn't have the finances that they needed, and sometimes I would retreat within the poverty of myself.

But when I walked in with the promises of God fresh in my mind, he would direct me to which needs to meet. A quiet confidence that God was at work filled me. He was sufficient for the needs that he wanted me to meet. I glimpsed the reason behind Calvin's emphasis on election. We do not have to meet the world's needs. The Holy Spirit will choose people's needs for us to meet.

Fear would be replaced with quiet confidence and trust in the all-loving and almighty Father. In this is rest. And God did protect. Only one person ever got angry with me in the community.

One day I was talking with a mechanic friend who had constructed a three-wheeled motorcycle. He offered me a ride. As we rode by, a drunken bystander on the footpath apparently called out and asked me to take him with me. I did not hear him. Later, when I returned, he came over and began to talk with me. He was angry, but since I couldn't follow his Tagalog, I didn't realize just how angry he was. Kid, my friend, stepped in and quieted him down.

Later that afternoon the drunken man took the motorcycle and smashed it. He knocked his head badly, and his concussion took two months to heal.

The people in the barrio said that his accident was a direct result of God protecting me. I was his servant, and fear came on the community! I didn't try to change their conviction that God had protected me. I *knew* that he had. That morning he specifically spoke to me of his protection from Psalm 91:14: "Because he cleaves to me in love, I will deliver him; I will protect him, because he knows my name."

Some time later, we prayed for the full recovery of the man who had smashed the motorcycle.

In incidents like this, I discovered the literal truth of the Apostle Paul's words: "For we wrestle not against flesh and blood, but against principalities and powers and spiritual wickedness in heavenly places," (Ephesians 6:12, author's paraphrase) so that "the weapons of our warfare are not physical weapons of flesh and blood" (2 Corinthian 10:4, Amplified) such as the weapons of the businessman, the politician, or the Church dignitary, "but mighty before God for the overthrowing of strongholds." Although opposition may come from people like this man, we know that our battle is against another.

NOTES

1. Toyohiko Kagawa, *Songs from the Slums* (SCM and Cokesbury Press, 1935).
2. A scholarly historical and doctrinal survey of views about revival is given by Richard Lovelace, *Dynamics of Spiritual Life* (Paternoster, 1979). Andrew Murray in 80 pages of notes at the back of *The Spirit of Christ* (Bethany House, 1984), gives the most comprehensive biblical theology of the Spirit capturing both Reformed theology, Keswick theology, the influences of the Welsh revival, and his own insights from the center of the South African revival.
3. A motivating book on this principle is by Alan R. Tippett. *People Movements in Southern Polynesia* (Moody Press, 1971).

Chapter Nine

Breaking the Poverty Cycle
PREACHING THE GOSPEL TO THE POOR

I had been in the community three months, and had spent most of that time praying. With a foundation for ministry already laid in prayer, it was time to begin preaching.

I needed to go up and visit the new converts among the Ibanag people, so I prayed for an evangelist to live in my house while I was away. Two days later, Jun and Milleth Paragas came to visit me.

Years earlier, we had worked together to plant a church. I had watched as the Lord gave and developed the gift of evangelism in Jun. He is a man of God, a Bible school graduate from a farming family. Milleth is a petite, charming Filipina, a trained singer, and a joyful wife.

This time, they came to Tatalon for counsel about a problem. While we discussed the problem, I had an idea.

"Why don't you stay in my house for a couple of weeks while I am away and look after it for me?" I asked. "You will have time to sort through your problem, and you can do some evangelism while you are here!"

They discussed the proposal together and decided to stay. They have stayed ever since!

For two months after I returned from my trip, we lived together in the same two cramped rooms. Then we found a house by the cliff, above the polluted river that circles around Tatalon. It had only one room. Foul smelling mud covered the floor. But outside, between house and river, lay a large expanse of land twenty feet wide, ideal for children and ministry activities.

The fellowship of his sufferings

After planting a garden on the land beside the house, we laid concrete on the floor to get rid of the smell of mud. Then we built a small bench, and bought a small gas tank and some cooking pots for Milleth. I offered to pay for all the food in exchange for Milleth's cooking.

Meals were times of deep fellowship together. As we ate our rice and fish for breakfast together and shared our struggles, I began to learn what Paul meant when he talked of sharing in the fellowship of the sufferings of Christ. (See Philippians 3:10.)Each morning one of us would be discouraged. It was not easy for Milleth and Jun to live in such a community. They had been moving up socially, in status, and economically. To become a squatter was to become a nobody.

One day, Jun came in, excited from his time down on the riverbank where he had been reading his Bible in the early morning sun.

"I've finally understood why we're living here!" he exclaimed. "I've just read 2 Corinthians 8:9. You know what it says? 'Jesus though he was rich, yet for our sakes became poor, that through his poverty we might become rich.'"

His enthusiasm was contagious. Milleth and I felt our spirits lift.

Our breakfasts became a communion meal where, together, we knew the cup of suffering and the bread of the broken body of Christ, as we uplifted one another. But it was a suffering with joy. James says: "Count it all joy, my brethren when, you meet various trials, for you know that the testing of your faith produces steadfastness. And let steadfastness have its full effect, that you may be perfect and complete, lacking in nothing" (James 1:2–4).

Only this spirit of joy in suffering—this knowledge that "It has been granted to you, for the sake of Christ, that you should not only believe in him, but also suffer for his sake"

(Philippians 1:29)—can in all honesty invite others to the task of identification with the poor.

Bible studies in the front yard

We decided that on Sundays at four o'clock in the afternoon, as the sun grew cooler, we would go through the Gospel of John.

Each Sunday morning we prepared songs and charts and invited all the neighbors to come to Milleth and Jun's home in the afternoon. As the shadows grew longer, about 30 adults and twice as many children brought wooden seats from their houses to sit around the blackboard. We sang together for a long time.

The first day, I experienced a wonderful freedom to preach in Tagalog. I began in Genesis and worked through to Revelation, very simply portraying fourteen events through the Scriptures. Because of their Catholic heritage, the people could identify with each story.

As I talked about the cross, the group fell silent. The Holy Spirit was clearly convicting them. I described how the Holy Spirit came to those who believed and repented.

The finale of the Scriptures captured their imaginations. They saw what the return of Jesus would mean for the poor. Even now, God was preparing a place for them, and justice would be done. They delighted in these promises of hope. The gospel is good news for the poor!

The archetypal Filipino personality has a romantic, idealistic streak in it and is easily captured by fantasy. The Filipino mind can easily understand a hopeful future. But what about their problems in the here and now?

They began to ask questions. Somebody asked on behalf of Aling Nena, "Do I need to give up my gambling if I am to go to heaven?" I threw the question back to the crowd. Another, now very interested, asked, "How do I know if I have the Holy Spirit?"

Someone else asked, "Do you mean that even a bad man who believes can have his name written in the book of life?"

As they asked questions, we discussed the Scriptures and the promise of grace in Christ. Milleth, Jun, and I began to experience the joy of seeing the gospel penetrate the daily reality of our neighbors.

The tide breaks

John the Baptist came preaching, "If you have two shirts, give one to the person who has none" (Luke 3:11, author's paraphrase). One of our professional friends took John the Baptist seriously and sent some clothes to Tatalon. We decided to give them to Kid.

Kid was the chief drunkard in the community. He was known as "Number One"—a big man, tough, yet wonderfully sensitive and intelligent. He had lost his wife a few years earlier and had never recovered. Instead, he had turned more and more to drink. But God had plans for Kid.

On Christmas Day, I invited him up to the house to give him the clothes donated by our professional friend. I could tell that he was already drunk.

Sitting on the small step between my kitchen and my bedroom, tears welled in his eyes.

"Nobody else gave me a present this Christmas," he said. He wanted to do something in return. We talked for a long time and he told me of the terrors of being a drunkard. He invited me to come to his home on the following day.

When I went, he was not there. He was drunk. Each day after that as I would enter or leave the community, I would pass Kid. He would be with a different barkada, always drinking. He would call me over and then introduce me to his friends.

"This is Viv, Brother Viv. He is a missionary and a good friend. You are to look after him." Then he would introduce his friends one by one and I would shake their hands.

Kid would say, "He's going to have a Bible study with all of you." We would sit and talk a little, and then I would continue on my way. Through Kid, I became acquainted with many families in Tatalon.

Jesus-style evangelism

Pastor Jun and I were born on the same day—December 26. To celebrate, we asked the ladies next door to make sandwiches and *pancit* (noodles). We invited all the neighbors to come and join us for our birthday party. We sang and we ate. The children came, enjoying the meal of pancit, sandwiches, and juice.

I stood up, sang in Tagalog, and gave my testimony. It was the best birthday I have ever had. It was also Jesus' style of evangelism—often in the context of feasting! Jesus tells us about birthday parties: "But when you give a feast, invite the poor, the maimed, the lame, the blind, and you will be blessed, because they cannot repay you. You will be repaid at the resurrection of the just" (Luke 14:13–14).

Jesus also talked about fasting. Perhaps he meant the kind of fasting that Isaiah describes. Fasting is to wander around the streets of your city and go and find a beggar, a drunkard, or an old lady and eat lunch with them. This is the kind of fasting that God wants:

> Is it not to share your bread with the hungry, and bring the homeless and poor into your house; when you see the naked to cover him . . . then you shall call, and the LORD will answer; you shall cry, and he will say, Here I am. (Isaiah 58:7, 9)

Fasting and feasting—Jesus' style of evangelism!

Noisy neighbors

One of the first people to experience the gospel breaking the poverty cycle was Aling Nena—my landlady.

Aling Nena ran a gambling den below my bedroom. She took a *tong* or a percentage each night as her income.

One night I was woken by men arguing over who would go home first. The one who had won a thousand pesos dared not go, lest he be stabbed by the others. Aling Nena was also shouting. She wanted them to go so she could sleep. Finally, they went—the winner first, the others some time later.

My diary for the next evening recorded the following: "Today Aling Nena is drunk. She wants to drown out the arguments from last night. She drank all morning and now she's shouting at Eleanor her daughter. Eleanor shouts back. Eleanor left later in the evening to sleep in another house to be free from the argument. I prayed, 'Lord, bring Aling Nena to a knowledge of yourself, for I cannot cope with living above such a gambling den. I need more sleep.'"

While I was away on a trip, Pastor Jun gathered the whole family and preached the gospel to them. Several believed, including Aling Nena. At first, she closed down the gambling den. But without gambling, she had no money, so she went back to her gambling business.

We helped her to set up a small *sari-sari* store. A *sari-sari* store sells a little bit of food, a little bit of this, a little bit of that. But Aling Nena was too generous, and gave everything out on credit. Within a short while, the capital was gone. Back to her gambling Aling Nena went.

One evening, at the time everybody sits on their haunches and relaxes after a day's work, Aling Nena and I sat in the cool shadows and talked about Proverbs 31. She heard the description of a godly woman, an older woman respected as a leader in righteousness in the community. She understood.

From that day on, she stopped her gambling, began to live righteously, and taught her children to do the same. Aling

Nena was the key to a whole extended family. Her friends were gamblers and powerful men throughout the community.

However, God blessed that evening conversation even more. As we sat talking, Aling Nena's niece joined us. She was waiting to go overseas to work in Hong Kong and had been working as a shop assistant in a store. She spent all of her income to process papers to go but had been waiting for months and months.

One of the evils of the poor is the exploitation by export agencies who call themselves "recruiting agencies." They make exorbitant sums of money for this trade in human flesh—which is legal. Perhaps this whole process of exporting labor should be developed along Christian lines in the way William Booth had proposed in *In Darkest England and the Way Out*. He sought to export people to the English Colonies of Australia, New Zealand, and South Africa. Should we not set up a Christian agency to do the same, and do it justly and honestly, without kickbacks, corruption, evil, and slavery?

Despite the exploitation of these export companies, it made more sense for Edith to try to go to Hong Kong and earn dollars than to remain in the poverty of Tatalon. Any hope is better than hopelessness.

Edith has a son. That evening, we talked about raising her son as a man of conviction and how the Bible was central to building this inward character in his life since he had no father. She understood, and her joy overflowed. She asked me for a Tagalog Bible.

Edith had given up her room for me when I first came. God had now returned her gift with his overwhelming generosity.

Drinking men's Bible study

In Tatalon, drinking with friends is a way to fill up the day and drown out the sorrow, the despair, and the insult to manliness inherent in unemployment.

As I walked through the community day after day, I watched groups of men sitting around on benches, with bottles of beer and small snacks shared between them. Those that had worked that day would share their money in order to provide the drinks for that evening.

I began to pray for the drunkards who would sit in front of our cluster of homes. As I went to my toilet, where I would wash each day from a bucket, I walked through this group of men and greeted them. Sometimes I stopped to sit and talk.

There was one man who was totally destroyed by his continual drinking. I cared for him, loved him, and talked with him. Aling Nena rebuked me.

"Bale wala iyon!" (He's worth nothing!), she said, telling me not to waste my time. Nevertheless, God cares for the drunkards.

One night, I came home late. As I walked down the road, I passed group after group of drinking men. When I clambered up the stairs to my room, I saw the men in my group had gathered in the next-door room upstairs where another couple lived. They were all drinking.

I boiled some hot water, made a cup of tea, and went in to join them. We talked and joked together for a while.

Then someone asked me, "How do you know there is a God?"

In broken Tagalog, I told them my experiences of God. They listened as they got more and more drunk.

"Are you a Catholic priest?"

"No, I'm a member of an order which establishes Bible studies and helps people come to a personal relationship with God. We help them apply the Bible to everyday life."

We talked and talked until they were too drunk to understand, and I slipped off to bed.

I was glad to establish rapport with these fellows. Later, when they were sober, we would talk more personally. Then I would build on this rapport and communicate the gospel more clearly. I began to pray particularly for this group of about fifteen drinking men. I would smile at them, love them, and wonder how we could introduce them to a Bible study.

Murderer!

Proverbs tells us, "The violence of the wicked will sweep them away" (Proverbs 21:7). Many of the wicked in a society are swept into the slums. Poverty is an environment for murder.

Several people had been killed in Tatalon. We would avoid one track home at night because there had been several murders there.

One day, I was talking with my drinking friends. We were sitting on some benches they had set out in the sun on the dry earth between the houses. This open space served as meeting area, children's playground, and a place for hanging out washing. I began to talk with a stranger, who seemed to be a friend of theirs. We started discussing religious topics. We had some friendly give and take, and I tried to lay the groundwork for further sharing.

Gary came over to me afterwards.

"Be careful with that one," he warned. "He is a professional killer. You know the shooting you heard last night?"

"Thanks, Gary. I didn't realize that!" I was humbled again at God's leading. By his grace, I had spoken gently to this murderer.

An old guitar

I wondered why there was so little music from a people who are reputedly so musical. Finally, I realized they didn't have guitars. I bought a guitar that I could lend to the group of men who sat outside drinking.

141

One half-destroyed young man would come regularly to borrow the guitar. I trusted him with it, and he considered this a high honor. I was one of the few people who had trusted him.

On New Year's Day, I returned from celebrating with the staff of the mission group. It was early in the morning, and the mist still clung to the river.

The men had stayed up all night and were still singing songs. One of them, Junior, was married to a woman working as a maid in Hong Kong. She sent money back to Junior to support him. The men wanted Junior to tape songs for her and send them to her on cassette. They had no tape recorder, but that didn't matter! They were sitting singing Filipino love songs.

As I sat down to relax with them, I asked, "Might I sing you a love song from New Zealand?"

I sang one or two Maori love songs, and then a Filipino love song. I passed the guitar to the man sitting beside me. Somebody brought us all some food to eat. I sat, singing, laughing, and enjoying the dignity and hospitality characteristic of Filipino people. Love for them seemed to overflow in my heart. I asked, "We would like to have a Bible study with you guys, drinking men only!"

They responded to the idea with a lot of humor. Pastor Jun joined us, and we discussed the idea. The consensus was that we would meet at seven o'clock on Sunday morning before anybody drank. They could not join the study if they had already had something to drink. Pastor Jun would give the necessary leadership to the group—my language was not yet fluent enough.

And so our drunkards' Bible study began.

We learned that these men did not enjoy a polite intellectual discussion about the Word of God. They wanted us first to teach them, and we would use all the authority and teaching skill we could muster. After the teaching, they would discuss if what was said was true and debate the application of the verses.

These men cared for each other. If one could not grasp what was being said, the others would teach him or would argue with him until he understood and believed.

A few weeks after the Bible study had begun, I returned to the neighborhood from a teaching trip to the province. I was walking down the concrete paths carrying my little bag when I felt a hand reach out and shake mine and heard someone say, "Hello, brod."

I looked into a smiling face. It was Gary. None of these men had called me "brod" before. My mind searched its files vacantly, desperately trying to understand the hidden meaning in these words, fighting hard to protect myself from another culture shock.

A second man joined him, smiling at my confusion.

"Can you get me one of those Bibles, the easy-to-understand one?"

Finally, I understood what they were trying to tell me. I laughed with joy, enthusiastically shaking the hands of my new brothers. While I had been away, Pastor Jun had set up an evangelistic meeting to which 400 people came. These men had entered the kingdom of God.

The kingdom had come to Tatalon.

Our cathedral

As the numbers of believers grew, we were determined not to waste money on a church building. If we ever constructed a building, it would be related to vocational training or socio-economic development.

But we grew to love our "cathedral" in Tatalon. It was magnificent, with its beautiful blue roof miles above us and God's dusty patchwork on the floor. We even had air-conditioning—the wind and the Holy Spirit blew where they would.

Our "overhead transparencies" were a large sheet of four-by-eight-foot paper with songs written on them in Tagalog. The preacher's lectern was a notebook in his hand. Instead of comfortable pews with cushions, we had wooden benches brought from each house by the people to sit on.

But most importantly, God was there in a way I've rarely known in some of the architectural monstrosities I've visited. Emmanuel attended—God with us, God who dwells among the poor.

Emerging fellowship

From this point, the fellowship of believers in Tatalon began to grow. The story from here on is not my story, but that of my co-laborers, Jun and Milleth. But let me outline its main thrusts.

I had tried to identify with the culturally accepted role of a priest, describing myself as a "brother" in a "movement which has Bible studies to help people come to know God."

Two main thrusts made up the ministry. The first was the Bible studies with the barkada—the groups of unemployed men and their drinking companions. The second was Bible studies to extended families.

As more and more people came to believe, we delayed baptism and distinctly Protestant worship. Baptism and worship services are seen as Protestant activities. Baptism is not seen as a symbol of conversion from sin, but as a symbol of conversion to Protestantism. We delayed baptism in order to maintain open links to non-Christian Catholic folk until there were believers in each segment of the community.

Rather than assembling people for worship, we had fellowship meetings once a month, each creative and broad in approach. These gradually drew together the Christians into a sense of identity—not within a Protestant church, but around the Lord they worshipped.

Discipleship and training in evangelism developed from the worship here. Often young men would oscillate between prayer meetings and drinking sprees until, step by step, as we met with them morning by morning in "group quiet times" (times of prayer and Bible reading), they came to deeper commitment.

I wasted a lot of time seeking to develop Tagalog materials for the Bible studies, only to realize that the culture of the poor is not a reading-studying culture. We needed to work directly from the Scriptures.

Despite not being able to read well, people devour comics. Comics cost only one peso each. I asked the Lord for the personnel to develop the Bible into comic form. A friend began to help with money given to us by a businessman, but my leaders rightly advised that the whole project was beyond our capacity at the time.

But as they became believers, they expected us to give them Bibles. How could we provide Bibles for the poor? Whole Bibles cost 38 pesos ($4 US)—a small fortune for the poor! If we sold them, people would become suspicious that we were using evangelism as a moneymaking venture. We tried numerous ways of overcoming this barrier, but until now, we have found no solution except to give or sell them at a small sum.

The coming of the middle-class

The believers multiplied. Over a period of several months, God led middle-class friends to the area one by one. They came saying, "God has called me to Tatalon." One of them was Theresa.

If Theresa hadn't responded to the call of God to the poor of Tatalon, she would have been completing her Masters degree in Manila's top management school. Instead, here she was killing cockroaches! Killing cockroaches takes time and this worried her top-flight executive mind. There were twenty details to be accomplished in finalizing an export link-up to New Zealand, in completing an audio-visual on the squatter ministry, and in assisting a new missionary friend to adjust.

I had received a vision concerning her—how she would choose between leading a lonely pioneering life in the slums or marrying a rich man. After a few weeks of working together, I told her about it. With a smile, she told me her story.

"I was molded for many years by my boyfriend," she said. "He was not a Christian, and I knew our relationship was wrong. Finally, I broke it off. That is the rich man. It was after this that God called me to the slums."

God had been speaking and that is a difficult thing to ignore— not to mention the more immediate voices of the team cheering her on! Theresa was the first woman (after Milleth) from the middle class to stay for more than a few days in Tatalon.

Worship

One Wednesday, a band of highly intelligent, committed professionals sat around a room praying and planning. The first phase of the work in Tatalon was almost complete. God had brought a ministry team together. After two years, the Lord had sent a number of these professionals to the slum to develop a discipling movement among the poor. And sitting beside them in worship were now a band of young Christians from Tatalon, some of whom were taking leadership roles.

Johnny, a salesman and graduate of the University of St. Tomas, one of Manila's top universities, had a gift of praying for the sick. God healed through his prayers.

Resty delighted before the Lord in praise, reminding the Lord of the great issues facing the country, asking that he might be faithful to his call to poverty, and begging for success with the economic projects God had gifted him to develop.

Pastor Jun Paragas took up the same theme with the Lord, his prayer reviewing the call, the costs, and the sacrifices for each one, asking God to extend and develop the next steps in evangelism, praising him for newfound patterns of worship.

Brother Romy, the engineer, prayed quietly, logically—the strong, silent, structural thinker, with a dream from God to be a church-planter.

Ofilia added her requests for the medical team she had been organizing.

Young Bien, who would go through deep suffering in years to come, lifted his heart in adoration for the Lord's encouragements to him.

Luz thanked God for showing her his love when her husband-to-be was far away. She had come for training in preparation for a life among the rural poor.

Milleth worshipped before the Lord in words reflecting the music of a soul deeply sensitive to him, thanking him for giving us the Tagalog songs we had been searching for.

Emy, the brilliant five-foot-tall theologian (was Paul like this?), was away on ministry to students. We prayed for him. Two years before he had been unable to come and join me, needing to care for his family. But God had not been still in his life. Finally he wrote the most beautiful letter to his church requesting them to release him to minister to the poor.

We began to pray for the coming weekend's activities.

A weekend in Tatalon

Mang Ekyu had just begun to climb into a tricycle when, from inside the tricycle, a blade flashed. He felt something warm push by his stomach, as he fell back and the attacker pushed past him. Blood!

"Quick!" he told the tricycle driver. "Get me to the hospital!"

A few days before, I had given his wife a cassette recorder and some tapes of Tagalog songs and the Gospel of John.

On Saturday night, we sat by his bed as he told us his story. He tried to tell it in English as Sally and Euan, New Zealanders on two-month cross-cultural trips, were with me.

I talked with him about Lazarus and the rich man, and the two ways that men go after death.

"That's right," he replied. "If a man is good he goes to heaven; if he is bad he goes to hell. You know, I have not been to church for many years. The reason is this. When a child is baptized, you pay the priest! When you get married, you pay the priest! When you die, you pay the priest! But what if you are poor?"

Jun and Milleth arrived opportunely, to finish sharing the gospel. I accompanied Sally back to Valenzuela—two hours across town. Women do not travel alone in Filipino society, especially at night.

I returned home at 10:30 PM. Resty and Emy had been waiting for me since five o'clock, when we had planned to discuss the theology of poverty. I felt like a failure. I had been unable to provide the necessary hospitality, and it was their first time in Tatalon. We rolled out our sleeping mats and mosquito nets. They slept, while I spent some time preparing for the worship and the seminar on disciplemaking that would take place the next day.

Worship usually began at 8:30 AM on Sunday. It was free flowing. We prayed and sang; Milleth sang as we prayed. Another sang his testimony and wept. We felt the presence of God so strongly that one young Christian began to confess his sin, and a drug addict asked God to take hold of his life before the power of drugs could take over again.

Each week, one of us would preach. Deeply burdened that Sunday, I preached for an hour.

Willie entered our "cathedral." We could all see that he was deeply upset. We sat silently, praying, and Johnny saw in his mind a picture of a gun.

"Willie," he asked. "Do you have a gun?"

Willie was startled! How did Johnny know? He began to share. The night before he had been with our friend Kid. Kid was drunk and would not accept Willie's refusal to drink. He began to curse Willie and insult him.

Willie went to his brother and brought back a gun and bullets. He was angry. But then something made him stop by the worship gathering.

After we heard his story, we talked and joked until the passion had died in Willie's eyes. He gave the bullets to Johnny. Never before had he been that close to murder.

Johnny was now in a dangerous position, since possession of bullets could be interpreted as subversion. The week before he'd dreamed of being in prison with some of the new believers. Perhaps prison would be sooner than expected! He took them and threw them in the river.

Just then, Mario brought Gary, a young believer, in to join us. Gary's eyes rolled and his body twisted—he was drunk. Gary had been the first to turn to Christ but had never fully renounced his drinking.

As we prayed for Willie, Gary joined in. He was so drunk, his prayer was only a quotation of the few Scriptures that he knew. Then, in tears and repentance, he told us his story. The night before, after drinking heavily, he had attacked his family with a *bolo* (a large machete). Fortunately, nobody was killed. Later, we would look back and see that this event and his repentance was the turning point in his life—the point of total commitment to Jesus Christ. After this day, he would follow the Lord wholeheartedly.

It was now lunchtime, and we had used up our discipleship training time in counseling. We were invited to a feast to celebrate the baptism of Frank's one-year-old boy into the Catholic church. Frank, Kid's brother, was a new Christian. We took Willie with us.

Frank's family served plate after plate of delicious Filipino food—hundreds of pesos' worth. His sister Fe was the cook. She came out, beaming at our obvious enjoyment over the feast. The week before, we had held a Bible study at her new house, immediately after the priest had blessed it.

We came back home to meet with the team and plan four events: the caroling, the Christmas party, Pastor Jun's birthday, and the dedication of their child. These upcoming celebrations would be a gathering for all believers.

The team then headed out to lead various Bible studies. I stayed back with some of them to teach them principles of leading a Bible study.

Confrontation with demons

Johnny went out with Emy to visit Willie's family. Emy, after two years of studying the theology of poverty, returned with a flabbergasted look on his face. None of the standard theological books had talked of being face-to-face with demons!

Johnny had been praying for the health of each member of Willie's family. As he did so, he laid his hand on each one's head. When he came to pray for the girl who worked as a helper for the family, his hand was flung back by some powerful force from the girl's body. The girl ran screaming from the house, her hair standing on end. Johnny learned that the girl's mother was an *albulario*—one who heals the sick by herbs and spiritual power. She did not want to be released, so they didn't pursue it.

This was the fourth direct demonic encounter within as many weeks. The demons spoke in a way that clearly showed their fear of us—and their knowledge of how the Word of God was being preached throughout the community. Breaking the poverty cycle requires a breaking of these demonic powers over men and women.

Jun and Milleth, in taking on these demonic powers, had themselves come under severe demonic attack. Milleth had been hospitalized twice; Jun had been in a motorcycle accident; Jedidiah, their one-year-old son, had contracted measles. It was one thing after another!

As we had prayed together about the attacks against them, a picture came to my mind of an idol somewhere in the house. I asked all the residents of the house if they had any statues of saints. The couple in the room next door to Jun and Milleth had a whole gallery of idols. Since their child had also often been attacked, they had called in the local priest to cast out the spirit. He had blessed the saints instead! The couple eventually left the room to save their child, locking the door behind them. We prayed against these spirits and "bound" them in the name of Christ. After this, Jun and Milleth were freed from the attacks.

Jesus tells us, "Do not enter a strong man's territory unless you bind the strong man" (Mark 3:27, author's paraphrase). We need to be wary of entering communities where Satan has focused his power, unless we are able to bind those powers in the name of Christ.

The gospel is spread today just as in Jesus' day: "So they went out and preached that men should repent. And they cast out many demons, and anointed with oil many that were sick and healed them" (Mark 6:12–13).

Another new believer also had a spirit within him. Some years ago a Catholic priest gave him a *mantra* (a word or series of words with spiritual power) in Latin to use against enemies, to obtain women, and so on.

We needed to pray for his release.

Deliverance was coming to the community, but Satan was a kicking, fighting antagonist who would not lie down. Usually on Saturday evenings before a day of such ministry, he would attack violently with sickness. On Sunday evenings, strange events would occur in our small house. But he was never victor.

It was now about six o'clock on Sunday evening. My *inaanak* (God-son), arrived. He is a qualified engineer, and God had given him a desire to develop economic projects for squatters. The economic projects committee assembled in the large room Jun had built on as an addition to house the vermiculture project (earthworms). While the worms multiplied underground, we used the room as a lounge.

After the meeting, I had supper with Melly, Jun's sister, and Euan, my visitor from New Zealand, who needed a little companionship after a day in an environment where he could understand little. I left him relaxing with the piano accordion that had arrived with some boxes of goods from my church in New Zealand.

It was late, but I heard that Aling Nena was in hospital. Should I go and find out what was wrong, or wait until tomorrow? I went back to my room and prayed. James's words came to mind: "Religion that is pure and undefiled before God and the Father is this: to visit orphans and widows in their affliction" (1:27).

But it was past nine, and I couldn't bring my body and emotions to go out again. I decided to sleep. I hitched up the mosquito net to keep out the rats, cockroaches, and mosquitoes and slept deeply, disturbed only by a rat knocking a jar into our rice pot and by the joyful sound of a group of midnight singers next door.

My dreams were sweet ones. Two years ago, there could not be found a righteous person in this place. Today there were a number. Because of their prayers, the Lord might yet save Tatalon.

Would he answer our prayers for a movement of 1,500 to 15,000 squatters firmly established in the Word of God?

Chapter Ten

Am I My Brother's Keeper?

EXPERIMENTS IN ECONOMIC DEVELOPMENT

"You are not making a gift to a poor man . . . you are returning what is his . . . The earth belongs to all, not to the rich."—St Ambrose

I skipped over a mud puddle and flicked open my umbrella in deft Filipino fashion as the heavy rain spots began to splash on the road.

Aling Cynthia was just ahead of me. I shouted out to her, *"Saan kayo papunta?"* (Where are you going?)

"Sa trabaho! Ikaw?" (To work! And you?)

"Sa doktor." I showed her the skin rash on my hands and feet that had developed from bacteria in the polluted pump water. We walked and talked.

"You know, Viv, you have no real problems," she said.

Akala mo! (That's what you think!), I thought to myself.

"You have enough to live on," she continued. Since Mang Mario, her second husband, had a heart attack, everything had gone wrong. "You know how happy I used to be. Now I do not smile. For one year now, life has been so hard."

I remembered Aling Cynthia as the enthusiastic member of a Bible study group a year before.

"If only there was work," I said sadly.

We walked in the silence of sympathy. She knew that I knew she would be forced to go to prostitution to feed her three children.

"Yes," she said. "For one year now I have searched, but there are no jobs."

As I listened, I felt as if my heart was falling apart. I thought back to a conversation with a young man in a church back home, who had asked, "Is it true you can just pray and God will provide jobs for people?" I had answered, "Yes, I can pray and God will answer. His answer is you. You are to sell all your excess things, work hard and make enough money to give to developing work for these poor!"

"Oh, Cynthia," I said, "I will do all I can. You pray for me, too, that I can find some men who will set up industries here in the squatter areas. It is so hard."

Women need Jesus Christ to stay out of prostitution—*and* an alternative income.

The drumbeat

There is a drumbeat beating in my head day after day, a beat that impels me forward into long hours of discipline and constant work. It is the cry of those saved from their sin, only to be entangled again by that same sin—by the tentacles of their poverty, drawing them down, down, down, till they are totally lost to this earth.

We must work and direct our undivided energy and unflagging zeal to provide economic stability for these, our new brothers and sisters in Christ. Like Kagawa, we must avoid being so busy working among the slum people that we forget to deal with the problems of the slums themselves.

Frank read the Tagalog Old Testament in three weeks after he was converted. He had time since he had no work. He was hungry for God. But without work, he sat around all day, and the pressure from his barkada became too much. He returned to his drinking. Drinking men need Jesus Christ—*and* a job.

We must not only evangelize and establish churches; we must also pastor these new believers. We must establish industries, act as social workers, and reform the structures that create their poverty.

Exploited workers need Jesus Christ—*and* assistance in the right ways to relate to their oppressive employers.

Oppressive employers need Jesus Christ—*and* teaching on how to repent of their exploitation and ill-gotten wealth.

City officials need Jesus Christ—*and* models on how to repent from corruption and utilizing their offices for their own ends.

The deserted wife, the pregnant girl, the disillusioned prostitute, the aged and ailing widow, the hungry child, the underpaid mother working to support a fatherless family all need Jesus Christ *and* . . .

> Evangelicals have always been suspicious of mission boards that concentrate on education, medical, social, or economic ministries, excluding or downplaying evangelism and spiritual development. Yet in most mission fields, one or more of the following conditions exist. If not attended to, they will inhibit the development of independent churches.
>
> Where public education is absent, church planting must include education to enable members to read the Scriptures.
>
> Where sickness and malnutrition sap energies beyond the struggle for mere existence, church planting must include public health and nutritional services.
>
> Where there is just enough food to survive, church planting must include agriculture and related sciences.

Where there is artistic or technical ability, church planting must include the development of these talents and where necessary the distribution of products.

Where small businesses are possible and needed, church planting must include training in business practices and perhaps even financial help.

The list could go on, depending on local conditions. In other words, to fulfill the church planting purpose of most missionary societies, a church planter must engage in more than evangelism and leadership training. Is it too hard a thing to say that it is criminal to go on establishing organized churches—churches that are condemned in advance to be permanently dependent on foreign money and personnel because we neglect the economic factors that would make self-support possible?[1]

The biblical response to poverty caused by sin is to preach the gospel to the sinner, but the biblical response to sin caused by poverty is to destroy the curse of poverty. Only when Christ returns will we fully be restored to our rightful role. But wherever his kingdom and righteousness take root on earth today, substantial restoration occurs and needs to be facilitated.

First steps

To an outsider, one area of need appears to be hygiene. The poor of Manila spend much of their income on highly paid doctors and on an exploitative, profit-making private hospital system. Over 90 percent of the poor have worms. Simple consistent teaching on basic hygiene needs to be an integral part of any growing Christian community.

We invited our friend Alan, a doctor, to come and teach the people about worms. He spoke first, on "How to get rid of the worms from your stomach," and then Pastor Jun spoke on "How to get rid of the worms from your soul."

If your people die young, of what value is your teaching?

Another friend, a university lecturer, began to join us once a week. Each time she came, she brought some herbal plants to add to the garden behind Jun and Milleth's house.

Within the folklore of the people, there are sufficient remedies from herbal plants for most complaints (including common colds) and to provide a nutritional diet. The Philippine Government has done sufficient research on their growth, traditional uses, and dosages.

All that is required is to find some representative of the poor, with the tenacity and desire to develop the model, plus someone to train such a person in basic horticultural technique.

In time, we expect to find such a man or woman.

Any cluster of squatter homes has enough walls and roofs to develop any number of window-box or pot-plant gardens. The potential from such a project in terms of herbal foods, medicines, hair shampoos and oils is well-known in Western countries. In time to come, God willing, a small-scale industry could easily be developed. The need is a man or a woman with the vision, the tenacity, and the willingness to learn the culture and develop the project over ten to fifteen years.

Why ten to fifteen years? Because most economic projects fail. An entrepreneur expects to fail and fail again until success comes. One research study analyzing 400 projects in the Philippines run by both the Government and private sector concluded that only 25 percent of these projects were moderately successful.

After discussion with experts in the field, I concluded that the basic reasons for failure are personal sin and the inability of the poor to manage finances. The sins include being too proud to feed the pigs, too lazy to water the plants, and harboring bitterness towards a member of the committee handling the project. Because of these attitudes, the gospel and the Word of God are basic to economic change. Spiritual and social healing provide basic ingredients necessary for economic success.

Rabbits are an interesting case in point. I tried rabbit projects at three different stages, but they require too high a level of technology and management for the average person in a squatter settlement. (Not to mention the fact that the word *daga,* rat, is also used for rabbit!)

Why did the rabbit projects fail? Small things are important in this type of business: cleanliness, care in feeding, detailed records for breeding and feeding purposes. When one litter of four-month-old rabbits is killed for meat, some of the money must be saved for feed until the next litter is killed. Someone without experience in keeping money—whose income each day is always insufficient—must learn how to save and invest. To succeed, the development worker would have to closely supervise the people, and I didn't have the time.

Pig-raising illustrates the same problem. Many people raise pigs. But a score of pig-sties lie empty and unused. The reason? A fiesta, a marriage, or a catastrophe. The pig is killed. The capital is gone.

Among those who have grown up in a "culture of poverty," there is usually little differentiation between capital, business finances, and personal needs.

Diet is another critical factor for the squatters. I found a group of nuns, "Sisters of the Good Shepherd," who had devoted their lives to developing suitable diets for the poor—nutritious diets within the incomes of the poor. Missionaries to the slums need to understand nutrition. Some need to teach it to others.

The diet of the poor is fish and rice—a diet greatly deficient in vitamin B as only polished rice is available. For this reason (apart from worms), many of the poor are anemic. Early on, Gene

Tabor had introduced REACH to brewer's yeast as a cheap way of avoiding this deficiency. *Mung* (mongo) beans supplement the protein requirements, but are also deficient in vitamin B. The poor in squatter settlements can learn to plant gardens that grow foods to balance their diets.

But gardens, goats, rabbits, and pigs do not provide a steady income. They merely supplement or maximize the use of available income. Their critical area of need is to find work, stable work, in industrial cities that do not have sufficient industry for its people.

The problem is not a new one. William Booth faced the same issue in London's slums a century ago. His solutions included matchmaking factories (from where we get the word "safety matches," which did not use the toxic, yellow phosphorous that caused death and sickness in many other factories), trade-training factories (an early form of sheltered workshop), farm colonies, and exporting men and women (after some skills training) to outlying British colonies such as New Zealand. Booth unfortunately died before implementing the last program.

Our first problem was not finding steady income for squatters, but to find a steady income for Pastor Jun, so he could be a self-supporting evangelist. Both of us knew that any discipling movement in the slums could not be dependent on foreign funding for its leadership. The squatter people needed a model of a pastor who, like Paul, was able to support himself with his own hands.

The first project Jun attempted was selling school supplies (notebooks, pencils, erasers, and so on) under contract to an aid organization working with 400 women in the community. This was a full-time project for three weeks before the school term. It provided enough income for three months. What Jun and Milleth needed, however, was an *ongoing* means of earning an income. Continuing to sell school supplies was a possibility, but few in our community had money or demand for them. A time might come in the future, as the community continued to develop economically, when a market for school supplies would be a reality, but at this time, it was not.

We needed a cottage industry with marketing possibilities outside of the squatters—among the middle-class or in the export market. Pastor Jun and his neighbors did a feasibility study of a bicycle assembly shop. They felt it might work, but with a very low profit margin. Success would be dependent on excellent management. Because of this, we were advised to try another approach.

Many ideas were suggested, and we debated and discussed their pros and cons. Finally, we agreed on vermiculture, or the growing of worms. With the help of an exporter, we would sell the worms to Japan, Canada, and Italy, where they would be used to make perfumes, placed in wines to make "macho" drinks, and eaten in worm-burgers! Their castings would make excellent potting soil for sale to rich people growing orchids.

Jun started with a few kilos of worms and worked diligently. The number of worms doubled each month. After a year, he had enough worms to begin selling. Unfortunately, at about that time, the exporter quietly packed up his office and disappeared. Jun, exhausted by the work, gave up. Where could he sell kilos of earthworms if not to Italians for perfume, Canadians for fish, or Japanese for burgers?

We went back to our discussions.

A good man

A man in Tatalon has outdone many Christians in his service to the poor of the slums—a small man, clad casually in shorts, and very intelligent. He owns a small joinery in Tatalon employing twenty workers. He buys cheap wood, builds cheap furniture, uses cheap transport (a horse and cart), and is kind to his workers. He has a degree in commerce.

The twenty men working there are the local drinkers. He pays them relatively low wages, but he provides stable work and often provides piecework for their children and wives. It is better to have stable work than no work at all or insecure work.

The men respect him. He sits and drinks with them. They say he knows *pakikisama*—how to get along with people, how to be one of the boys. That's a high compliment for a man.

This is the kind of industry the squatters need: a place where men can learn a skill on the job in a productive business. Most unskilled men are unable to produce first-class work at an economic price. They have not enjoyed the benefits of training and education needed to become skilled craftsmen. Economic aid has to be focused at the level of developing entrepreneurs who will take others with them as they move out of poverty.

A friend came to help with some electronics ideas. Another friend told of someone who was employing several squatter Christians in a shoemaking project. Starting a welding shop seemed like a good idea since there were many jeepney and tricycle body-building shops throughout Manila. Each project required a skilled person to develop and manage it.

Over a period of time and the study of various economic projects developed by other groups, a conviction grew that with a team of three people with the right skills, a cottage industry-skills training project would succeed. For example, a woman trained in marketing, an engineer trained in production, and someone with management skills would be able to handle most projects. Three people seemed an appropriate number in a consensus-oriented society.

It also was obvious that the West is full of down-to-earth, practical men and women who, with little equipment, can build most things they need. They have imbibed basic management skills from their culture. I began to pray for such people in their late thirties to forties: people with above average sensitivity, able to stick at such projects for sufficient time until the culture is mastered and the work established, who can hold a hacksaw in one hand and a Bible in the other—who can, as they pass on skills, also pass on the love and power of the God at work within them. Grey-haired, retired executives would be a special gift from God. In the role of economic development consultant to the slum community, a skilled person could even work from outside the slum.

Will renewal become revival?

Our minds are saturated with data contrasting rich nations with poor. We do not want to hear any more of the problem. Most Western Christians long to hear of potential *solutions* that they can be involved in.

The church in New Zealand has had a deep social conscience concerning the Two-Thirds World poor. During the sixties and seventies, a significant percent of non-Christians in New Zealand defined a Christian as someone who does good for his neighbor, gives to the poor, visits prisons, and so on.

Partially, they were right. Faith without practical evidence, according to both Jesus and James, is not faith at all. Evangelicals often define the evidence of faith as baptism or a personal testimony (based on Romans 10:9–10). These are evidence. Jesus, however, adds another piece of evidence:

> Come . . . inherit the kingdom . . .
> For I was hungry and you gave me food,
> I was thirsty and you gave me drink,
> I was a stranger and you welcomed me,
> I was naked and you clothed me,
> I was sick and you visited me,
> I was in prison and you came to me.
> (Matthew 25:34–36)

While on furlough, I felt constrained to declare that unless the cleansing and renewal occurring in New Zealand churches resulted in an economic repentance, it would not be true revival.

Affluence and worship do not result in pleasure to God. A new spirituality must be outworked in new economics. Raised hands, ecstatic spiritual experiences, and new worship forms in dance and music on their *own* are of no consequence to God. They are not holy but like a mud bath in his sight *unless* accompanied by economic repentance and justice. Listen to Isaiah: "Bring no more vain offerings; incense is an abomination to me. New moon and sabbath and the calling of assemblies—I cannot endure iniquity and solemn assembly" (Isaiah 1:13).

Renewal came to New Zealand. Thousands of new house groups developed a distinctly effective Kiwi model of evangelism.

But Western nations must follow the model in Acts, when the coming of the Holy Spirit was followed by economic repentance and new economic structures.

Acts Chapters 2 and 4

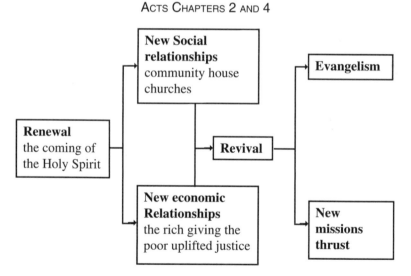

First, at a house group and church community level, a commitment to economic sharing is necessary and, through this, a commitment to a simpler lifestyle. This will be the basis of a ministry of integrity to the poor.

Second, as a poor class emerges in the West as a result of economic depression, churches need to be ministering to them, drawing them into extended families and establishing work schemes.

Third, in relationship to the Two-Thirds World, Western churches need to take leadership in national repentance for our continued exploitation of the Two-Thirds World's resources, our restrictive trade licensing system, our unjust balance of trade relationships with Two-Thirds World nations, and our totally inadequate aid policies. If the church does not repent, how can the government? The church is called to be the conscience of the nation.

Fourth, we need to get into the hands of the poor the means of production by:

(a) transferring our technical expertise through people who will give themselves long-term to learning another culture, identifying the level of local expertise, and passing on appropriate technology;

(b) donating or donating funds for the equipment needed to help Asia's urban poor begin small-scale industries; and

(c) getting funds to Asia's poor without interest and without unnecessary controls.

These constructive activities would all be components of economic repentance, repentance from the sins of Sodom:

> Behold, this was the guilt of your sister Sodom: she and her daughters had pride, surfeit of food and prosperous ease, but did not aid the poor and needy. (Ezekiel 16:49)

Traditional Western churches have rejected these words from God. In places where some have heard these words gladly and taken action, we can see a humbling before God and subsequent renewal.

May I have your sewing machine?

Ladies in the West often have two sewing machines. We asked them to give up one. I did not dare suggest that the rewards of giving their new one to be used full-time in the hands of a poor lady might outweigh the difficulties they would have going back to their old one. With two exceptions, we received old sewing machines.

My church in New Zealand is an unusual one. A number of wealthy executives, doctors, and professionals belong who have chosen simple homes and lifestyles, and who delight in supporting missionaries. They organized a "Day of Jubilee," bringing many goods for the poor as a sign of renewed commitment to simplicity. Nine crates of goods were marked for Manila.

Meanwhile, the team in Tatalon was planning what to do with the goods when they arrived. Theresa and Resty were both engineers who came to be part of an economic projects committee. We discussed what we would do with the welding machine and the sewing machines. Could we set up a carpentry shop for the four carpenters who had been converted? Theresa prayed for a pair of glasses for Kid, who had frequently said he was unable to read the Bible because of poor eyesight.

The goods arrived. Four days of sweat, clearance through customs (with no bribes!), and fifty-nine signatures later we were careening down the streets with our full load. Christians in Tatalon sorted and packed the clothing into plastic bags. Lo and behold, a pair of glasses! Only later did we discover that the church secretary in New Zealand had misplaced his glasses while packing the goods!

We went around the community singing, giving the clothes and shoes to the poorest widows and families. A young pregnant woman began to weep. "I thought I had no friends, nobody to love me," she said.

The sewing machines were spirited away to Aling Berta's house. Gary and Berta had been two of the first to believe and were recognized as leaders within the community. Berta was the daughter of our barrio councilor or community leader. She immediately set in motion her plan to employ some women in turning off-cut cloth into rags that could be sold to jeepney drivers. Other machines would be used in dressmaking.

Importing company

I wanted someone to grapple with the issues related to unjust trade practices. We also needed a cottage industry outlet from Manila. We prayed for an evangelical importing company to be established in New Zealand. (A large "alternative" importing group in New Zealand had begun from a Christian base but had become associated with Marxism. In the politically volatile situation of the Philippines, we couldn't risk working with them. Nonetheless, over the years this agency has brought about a significant number of creative changes in New Zealand's trading policies.)

I prayed for one year. A week before returning to the field, the house group of a friend volunteered to put up shares and set up such a company.

Four cottage industries exist among the 14,000 residents of Tatalon: carpentry, cane chair-making, crochet, and *burricraft* (a form of grass weaving). We spent many hours linking these up to a non-profit Christian exporting company and to the import company in New Zealand. Being involved in importing is giving the house group a first-hand opportunity to apply the biblical teaching on helping the poor and on doing justice.

Prayer and economics

But taking on Satan in the area of economics is not without spiritual opposition. Behind these activities were long evenings of prayer. The Lord made himself known during one particular evening in Tatalon. About twenty-five gathered together that night. How beautiful it was to hear Aling Nena pray in Tagalog!

"Lord, help us; we're just poor people, but we know that before you there's neither rich nor poor. We're very poor, so help us. Please heal me from my sickness. I believe in you. I haven't been to the *albulariol* (spiritualist or faith healer).

"And Lord thank you for hearing me—for giving work to Eleanor, my daughter. And I want to thank Viv for giving her the capital!"

We had given Eleanor 200 pesos of the capital given to us for exporting goods so she could begin running a meat stall in a market. She was repaying us 5 pesos per day, so we could recover the capital before the export goods left for New Zealand and use it for its designated purpose.

This loan system worked well. Other new believers asked if they, too, could take loans of 300 pesos, repaying them at a rate of 5 pesos per day after the first two weeks. The loans were repaid within three months. Helen borrowed money for a dried fish stall; Liz and Rene for an eatery; another for *bagoong* (a tasty sauce made from ground anchovy fish).

We discussed ways to improve the system. An economic committee was set up consisting of people from Tatalon. These were now their own projects—run with their own motivation. Control of the finances and economic development policy was now in their hands. The young fellowship was now establishing an economic identity reflecting principles of the kingdom!

And the future?

Dreams create work, so it is wise not to have too many. With a goal of assisting every squatter Christian leader to gain a skill or become self-supporting, dreams can be multiplied a hundredfold.

Soap-making, shoe manufacture, food stores, and beekeeping (there are only about 400 beekeepers in the Philippines) have all been suggested. Micro farms that integrate ducks, fishponds, rice, goats, pigs, methane gas production, and vegetables in a small area—and a multitude of other ideas—are all potential programs.

But they all come with costs in time, money, and management that have to be weighed and paid at the right season. Programs have to emerge from the felt needs and responses of the squatter Christians. They have to be developed by someone trained to manage, and such personnel are hard to find among the poor.

William Booth summed up his experience in the area of economic programs among the converted poor:

> Most schemes that are put forward for the improvement of the people . . . would only affect the aristocracy of the miserable. It is the thrifty, the industrious, the sober, the thoughtful who can take advantage of these plans . . . No one will ever make a visible dent on the mass of squalor who does not deal with the improvident, the lazy, the vicious, and the criminal. The scheme of social salvation is not worth discussing which is not as wide as the scheme of eternal salvation.

At the same time, he wrote:

> I would not disguise the fact that I attach far more importance to reform of the man than to reform of the law. The problem of problems lies here in a nutshell.[2]

The missionary role

What is the role of the pioneer missionary in all of these things? Missionaries will never become one of the people. They will always be guests in a culture despite mastery of language, understanding of cultural values, and depth of relationship.

The biblical word for *missionary* is apostle or sent one. Apostles are to pioneer, to reach into new areas, to establish new fellowships, laying the correct framework built on Jesus Christ. They must lead, set the pace, and preach the word. Apostles are to direct the new believers to study the Scriptures for solutions to their own problems. They are to sit and listen, clarifying the issues, but let the believers find their own solutions.

Local Christians understand the social structure, the economics, and the politics of life around them. They can bring socio-economic and political change within society. The missionary's role is to teach the breadth of Scriptures, to provide the depth of theology needed for a movement.

Western missionaries today must recognize at the same time that they are brothers and sisters to a nation of rich people. Behind them are great resources which, because of a commitment to justice and compassion, they must tap. And this requires management. Christian aid agencies are useful, with administrative structures already established to take Western money and give it to the poor.

Jesus lived simply, but he, too, had behind him infinite resources. The missionary is to initiate and yet must, at the same time, seek to remain free from the administrative and managerial load that each economic and legal project demands. We must be free to pioneer new ideas, recruit new laborers, delegate tasks, and set up the structures for them to function by; free to continue preaching the word and opening up neighboring communities to the gospel; free to live the carefree life so loved by a modern-day follower of Francis of Assisi.

The first apostles or church leaders were well aware of the tension between initiative and freedom. Initially, they had to handle the economic interchange between rich and poor inspired by the Holy Spirit. As time went on, they realized the need to delegate the administration of a program for widows to seven deacons (for *deacons* read social workers, community developers, or administrators): "Therefore, brethren, pick out from among you seven men of good repute, full of the Spirit and of wisdom, whom we may appoint to this duty. But we will devote ourselves to prayer and to the ministry of the word" (Acts 6:3–4).

They themselves would put priority on the spiritual dimensions. Jesus did the same thing constantly. I used to wonder why Jesus, a carpenter, never set up a carpentry-training program to help some of the poor. But he declared his vocation "to preach the gospel to the poor" (Luke 4:18) and called the disciples to "go . . . preach the gospel" (Mark 16:15).

Jesus knew that preaching the kingdom, confounding demonic powers, and healing the sick were priorities. He was hitting at the cancer in the core of society, not just the symptoms. Francis Schaeffer has described how theology influences philosophy, which then influences the arts and music, and, from this, all areas of life.

A matter of perspective

The squatter views his slum as a place of hope. The Western outsider views it as unsanitary, full of disease, lacking water, adequate housing, privacy, peace and quiet, trees, and so on. It appears destitute in comparison with the neighboring "normal" middle-class subdivisions that can be observed elsewhere. This point of view is only natural for the Westerner suddenly thrown into a shantytown.

In reality, the standard of living in most slums is no lower than in the rural areas from which the inhabitants have recently come, nor is it, perhaps, very different from that of the industrial West a century ago. But to modern Western eyes, life in the slum is in stark contrast with the technologically advanced, affluent urban populations in industrialized nations and, even more pertinently, with that of the elite of the Two-Thirds World.

For the slum dweller, life is much better than it used to be. Unlike residents in a more affluent subdivision, slum dwellers find cohesion and solidarity in their communities. Urban slums provide opportunity for him to participate in a new technological world: in consumer goods, a better educational opportunity for his children, and an increased average income over what he was able to earn in the province. The slum is a bridge to that long-hoped-for opportunity, a place to live close to kin, a way out of landlessness and exploitation.

Some may argue that we should not help the urban poor to move up, as they may move out of these areas. Apart from the obvious ethical fallacy in this statement, it is factually not true. About half of the areas identified by the government as squatter areas in Manila will be upgraded, and they have become stable places of residence. The entire community has the chance to move out of poverty together.

NOTES

1. Excerpts from Charles H. Troutman, "A Fallacy in Church Planting: a Fable," *Evangelical Missions Quarterly,* July 1981, 137.
2. General Frederick Coutts, *Bread for My Neighbor* (Hodder and Stoughton, 1978).
3. Maslow, Abraham Harold., *Motivation and Personality,* 3rd edition (Addison-Wesley Pub Co, 1987).

Chapter Eleven

With Justice for All

SQUATTER POLITICS

One day as I was walking down the road to my house, the leader of the women's group called out her greetings. I stopped, and we talked. She invited me in and began to tell me about an event that had taken place some years ago.

The landowner had ordered the squatters to be evicted many times. This time he brought both the court order and the local police chief. The squatters had been warned! Behind him came a bulldozer to push down the squatter homes.

The protest began. The people, screaming, lay down and kneeled in front of the bulldozer. Thugs hired by the landowner dragged them away.

A local priest arrived and tried to calm the people. He asked the bulldozer driver to be patient. The driver was angry, too, but quieted down. Police reinforcements arrived. The priest organized the people to lie down in front of the bulldozer. He spoke about non-violence. He talked with the police chief, informing him that the mayor had been called and would be arriving soon.

As a Christian called to work in the slums, what would you do when your people's homes are about to be destroyed? What would you do in response to violence, murder, oppression, and injustice? Does your heart burn with anger and reaction, with the desire to fight back and defend?

God feels the same way. He is a God of justice. He defends the poor and needy. In this case, the mayor defended the squatters' rights. Years later, they obtained legal rights to the land.

Just lifestyles

I stumbled across a small passage in Jeremiah 22:13–17. For years I had taught that the knowledge of God comes through Bible reading and prayer. These activities are certainly basic to all else. However, the logical outcome of such a doctrine was to spend more and more time in prayer and Bible reading and less and less in the activities of life. Ultimately, one becomes a hermit.

The verses in Jeremiah challenged me: "to know God" is "to do justice and righteousness . . . [to judge] the cause of the poor and needy."

A hunger for God throws us not into pietism, but into the thick of injustice on this earth.[1]

"Justice and righteousness" is a phrase similar to our concept of social justice. Perhaps, since the phrase "social justice" may have radical overtones, we might talk about living "just lifestyles." In whatever work or area of social responsibility we are involved, a just lifestyle requires bringing just dealings, creating just programs, reforming unjust practices, and standing against unjust actions.

A call for missionary servants

God is a God of justice. From these devastated masses of destitute humanity that are Manila's slums, three million cries for help and mercy reverberate around the throne room and entry halls of his court.

God hears! And he rises in indignation and anger!

He looks for one who will stand before him for the poor of this city. Two thousand years ago, finding none, he sent his own Son, declaring:

> Behold, my servant, whom I uphold.
> My chosen, in whom my soul delights;
> I have put my Spirit upon him,

He will bring forth justice to the nations.
(Isaiah 42:1)

Notice his choosing. Note his empowering. And note his purpose: a missionary call to bring forth justice to the ends the earth. Jesus repeated these thoughts in Luke 4:18, when he said the Spirit of the Lord was upon him to preach the gospel to the poor. Jesus' gospel was good news to the oppressed, good news of a kingdom where justice will reign. Note also the servant's methodology, his manner of bringing justice:

He will not cry or lift up his voice,
or make it heard in the street. (Isaiah 42:2)

God does not send high-flying diplomats on shuttle diplomacy. God's servant is not an articulate demonstrator, megaphone in hand. Or a flashy, traveling evangelist with glossy promotional materials.

He comes humbly, riding on an ass, washing others' feet, healing sword-cut ears. Isaiah tells of the Messiah's gentleness:

A bruised reed he will not break,
and a dimly burning wick he will not quench. (42:3)

He doesn't snap off those of us who are broken reeds, but gently binds us up. He does not snuff out, like a candlewick between his fingers, those who are almost burned out. Instead, he fans us back until we become a blazing light.

Such is God's method of bringing justice. And this justice is sure:

He will not fail or be discouraged
till he has established justice in the earth. (42:4)

We are his body, called to the same role as our Master. We are servants of the Servant.

"If anyone serves me," he says, "he must follow me; and where I am, there shall my servant be also" (John 12:26). How high a calling!

As the basis of his lifestyle, Paul claimed a passage from another one of these servant songs. It defined the task of the servant as follows: "My servant . . . I will give you as a light to the nations, that my salvation may reach to the end of the earth" (Isaiah 49:6).

We, too, are called to declare this salvation to the ends of the earth as God's servants. Incarnating God is to incarnate justice and righteousness in a servant lifestyle:

> For he delivers the needy when he calls,
> the poor and him who has no helper.
> He has pity on the weak and needy,
> and saves the lives of the needy.
> From oppression and violence he redeems their life;
> and precious is their blood in his sight.
> (Psalm 72:12–14)

Personal justice

There are four levels of doing justice: first, in personal dealings; second, in peacemaking, bringing reconciliation between parties; third, in establishing movements of people who live justly; and fourth, in causing change at the upper levels of society.

The first level of justice begins with the fear of the Lord—the Lord who hears the poor and acts on their behalf. This gives us a deep fear of offending or humiliating a poor man. Personal justice begins in small things. Once, I forgot to pay the girl from the squatter home next door. She typed for me two or three days each week. I had almost reached my destination in another province when I remembered: "Oh no, I forgot to pay my typist!" I felt a sinking feeling in my stomach as this verse flashed into my mind:

"You shall not oppress a hired servant who is poor and needy . . . You shall give him his hire on the day he earns it, before the sun goes down (for he is poor, and sets his heart upon it); lest he cry against you to the LORD, and it be sin in you" (Deuteronomy 24: 14–15).

In addition to justice in small things, personal uprightness in its biblical context includes social justice. Ezekiel describes the righteous person as one who: "does not oppress any one, but restores to the debtor his pledge, commits no robbery, gives his bread to the hungry and covers the naked with a garment, does not lend at interest or take any increase, withholds his hand from iniquity, executes true justice between man and man, walks in my statutes, and is careful to observe my ordinances—he is righteous" (Ezekiel 18:7–9).

Justice as peacemaking

Being rich among the poor, however, requires more than personal justice with a social component. In a situation of injustice and oppression, discipleship involves a second level of doing justice: peacemaking, bringing reconciliation between parties, seeking justice for those unjustly treated.

"Open your mouth, judge righteously, maintain the rights of the poor and needy," commands the King of Massa in Proverbs 31:9. Speaking out is dangerous. The disciple in the slums will alternately be labeled "CIA" or "Marxist," depending on who is against him. Neither label is correct, for we work not for the communist nor the capitalist cause. We work only to do the righteousness of the kingdom.

Consider the sad letter I received from my Filipina *kumadre,* my "blood sister":

> Eli has now no employer, so we are not earning even a single penny. We are just making a living through borrowing and debts. With regard to our

kids, they are often contaminated by common illnesses successively. You know, Viv, we do not know how to solve our problems. Incidentally, the government agency that owns our land is asking us to vacate the place where we are in for the reason of not remitting our payment since we have lived here.

I responded by helping them make their payment. Her next letter was even more troubling, and explained how the cost of 3,825 pesos for their house had now become 9,460 pesos over two-and-a-half years.

Doing justice in that case meant finding out whether this 300 percent increase in the price of a house was due to unjust policies written by the government or whether a corrupt official was behind it. Justice meant trying to rectify the situation. It meant giving to my brother and sister in need, never expecting it back. It meant finding work for my *kumpadre*. And where my lack of resources and time made all of this impossible immediately, it meant looking to God to bring his judgment on those who perpetuate such legal crimes. For God: "will not revoke the punishment . . . because they sell the righteous for silver, and the needy for a pair of shoes—they that trample the head of the poor into the dust of the earth, and turn aside the way of the afflicted" (Amos 2:6–7).

Injustice cries out from the land!

The servant missionary seeking to bring justice and righteousness to the people in the slum must understand the history of exploitation that forced the people there.

In the rural Philippines, the provinces' leading families, Spanish priests, American businessmen, and the Japanese war machine have all contributed to this poverty. Now, feudal barons who own the land farmed by tenants reinvest their profits in industry, land speculation, and multinational companies in Manila.

Eventually, the money is shipped out of the economy through the multinationals to the United States, Japan, and elsewhere.[3]

One day as I was out jogging in the Filipino countryside (sometimes I did culturally unacceptable things like jogging alone), I ran past the massive gates of a mansion. I stopped and peered through the gates at the grounds and the building, just visible behind the guards.

I jogged to a basketball court nearby and began talking with some local farmers. I asked them where their landlord had earned the money to build his mansion. They sat around on their haunches, joking back and forth about the question. In between the jokes (a way of covering embarrassment or shame), they told me how most of the local families gave 50 percent of their crop to the landlord. Before the land reform law was implemented, he used to provide them with help if they were sick or in need. Those that obtained ownership rights to the land no longer received such help in time of need. They were forced to go into debt to the money-lender, who charged a much higher rate than the landlord exacted. (For every five pesos, the lender receives six pesos the next day—this system is called "five-six.") Proverbs comments: "The fallow ground of the poor yields much food, but it is swept away through injustice" (13:23). Most poor farmers are constantly confronted with these injustices. But working in a government job does not guarantee fair treatment either.

One of our friends in the slum, Susan, moved into an accountant's position in the local municipal office. She soon discovered that her bosses "fiddled" the books for profit. The auditor was in the know and received his cut. The investigator from the Bureau of Internal Revenue was paid off when he came. How could Susan continue to work and maintain her integrity as a Christian? If she exposed the system or rebelled against it, she would lose her job.

Is God biased for the poor?

Does God have a bias for the poor? Is he involved in a class war? The Scriptures do not support a Marxist analysis of class war. In James 5:1–6, God *does* appear to have a bias for the poor, but only an *apparent* bias. God seems to prefer the poor only if we compare his care for them with our own lack of concern.

As a good father will protect his youngest from being beaten by his eldest son *precisely because* he is a good and just father, so God particularly prefers, protects, and identifies with the poor. But let us not call him partial. Although he is a compassionate God, we know that he is an impartial God. He treats *all* as of infinite value and worth.

But his compassion and justice compels his involvement with the less fortunate. He condemns the unconcerned, luxurious lifestyle and oppression of the rich. James says:

> Come now, you rich, weep and howl for the miseries that are coming upon you. Your riches have rotted and your garments are moth-eaten. Your gold and silver have rusted, and their rust will be evidence against you and will eat your flesh like fire. You have laid up treasure for the last days. Behold, the wages of the laborers who mowed your fields, which you kept back by fraud, cry out; and the cries of the harvesters have reached the ears of the Lord of hosts. You have lived on the earth in luxury and in pleasure; you have fattened your hearts in a day of slaughter. You have condemned, you have killed the righteous man; he does not resist you (5:1–6).

Justice in Christian community

The third level of doing justice in the slums is to establish movements of believers who:

(a) demonstrate justice in their lifestyles with each other

(b) begin to bring justice into the life and leadership of their immediate community.

Communal justice, like personal justice, also begins with small things. And all justice is rooted in prayer.

For example, God filled us with a desire to pray for an end to the unsanitary garbage in one part of the community. Garbage is a small issue, but seeking God's care in the small issues affects the community. An answered prayer gave us the freedom and respect to relate to community leaders and officials on more major issues such as when the landowners brought in bulldozers to push down homes.

Our responsibility was to become recognized spiritual leaders within the community. If we could establish trust and deepen our relationships day by day, the community might look to us and to God when they faced bigger issues.

Just lifestyles must be seen in believers first. The church must be established in justice as a reference point for non-believers. John Perkins describes the growth of a community of believers who demonstrated justice in their relationships to a racially torn community. Their dream was: "to carve out of the heart of Jackson, Mississippi, a community of believers reconciled to God and to each other. To bring together a fellowship of blacks and whites, rich and poor. Such could make a positive difference in the lives of a community enslaved by poverty and racism."[4]

But is it enough to demonstrate justice through holy living? Some see church planting as bringing a small group of believers out of a life of sin into the Kingdom of God. These believers stay in the community but live separate, holy lives.

Others view church planting as empowering believers to establish the kingdom of God within their community. Instead of believers entering the Kingdom of God and leaving worldliness behind, believers are encouraged to stay "in the world" and actively work to bring the Kingdom of God into their community.

Because of my Anabaptist and fundamentalist heritage, I focused on a separated group of believers during my first years of church planting. Such separated communities have, paradoxically, brought many major political changes into our own society. They can be true lights and bright beacons on a hill. Armed with a strong conviction of rescuing people from damnation, these Christians have often become deeply involved in the problems of their age.

Quakers developed the early mental hospitals; the Salvation Army pioneered the first sheltered workshop schemes; the Mennonites have consistently worked at peacemaking nationally and internationally. Early Anabaptists advocated separation of church and state, religious liberty, and the role of free choice in matters of faith, each of which became major political issues in their time.[5] Modern non-religious social work often imitates activities developed by such groups.

But as I listened to the urgent cries of the poor, and studied the writings of Booth, Kagawa, Calvin, and Wesley and their work among the poor, as well as the history of missions, my separatist missions strategy was challenged.

I pored over the Bible. Passages such as Proverbs 11:10–11, ("When it goes well with the righteous, the city rejoices . . . By the blessing of the upright a city is exalted") indicate an active involvement by the righteous in community leadership. God was leading me to a desire to establish the kingdom within every level of society—and, where the social structure permits (as in Calvin's Geneva or in last century Tonga), over society.[6]

We discovered a vital principle in Jeremiah's prophecy to the exiled Israelites when they were taken to Babylon: "Build houses and live in them; plant gardens and eat their produce. Take wives and have sons and daughters. . . . But seek the welfare of the city where I have sent you into exile, and pray to the LORD on its behalf, for in its welfare you will find your welfare" (Jeremiah 29:5–7).

As aliens and exiles looking towards our heavenly home, we must also seek the welfare of the cities in which we are living. Although our future in the kingdom is secure, we should not sit back and do nothing. We must obey our Master's command to love our neighbor and try to bring kingdom principles to bear on the structures of society around us.

Upper-class evangelism

To serve the poor, seeking personal justice, peacemaking justice, and communal justice are not enough. We must seek changes at the upper levels of society. But only a few of us are called to this task.

For most of us, God has called us to apprenticeship: to start where we are, take what we have, and do what we can at a community level. To do this, we might first establish communities of believers, alternative economic structures and small businesses, and then motivate local politicians to right decisions and confront local leaders with their wrongs. God may then give us grace for a wider field of ministry, but let us not be arrogant.

On the other hand, the few Christians of the upper class who have been committed to bringing the kingdom of God into or over every aspect of society have brought about fundamental social changes. The rich are the key to unlocking the poverty of the poor.

This is the cry of that famous passage in Isaiah 59:12–16, where the steps of social breakdown are described and the Lord cries for a man of justice:

> We know our iniquities . . .
> speaking oppression and revolt . . .
> Justice is turned back . . .
> for truth has fallen in the public squares,
> and uprightness cannot enter . . .
> The LORD saw it, and it displeased him that

there was no justice.
He saw that there was no man,
and wondered that there was no one to intervene;
[no intercessor].
Then his own arm brought him victory,
and his righteousness upheld him.

The most famous group of upper-class Christians in English history was the Clapham Sect, friends of William Wilberforce. They were influential noblemen, bankers, politicians, and industrialists in the late eighteenth and early nineteenth century.[7] At one time, they infiltrated and took over the entire directorate of the East India Company, using it to champion the rights of the native races! Their persistent advocacy of morality in all dealings with subject nations did much to create notions of trusteeship and responsible imperial government. The relief of debtors, the destruction of slavery, the mitigation of the savage eighteenth century penal code, the ending of discrimination against Jews, Catholics and Protestant dissenters, the provision of charity to the victims of the Industrial Revolution—these reforms and others like them are credited to these evangelists.

Today, God continues to look for leaders committed to such truth and justice.

Effective social change

If great social changes that help the poor are brought about by the rich, why work directly with the poor?

First, mass movements from the grassroots eventually produce changes in the top of society. The members of the Clapham Sect were the direct descendants of the Wesleyan revival. McLelland, in a significant study on entrepreneurs, shows that the two great waves of achievement in England were associated with Protestant reform or revival. Christians with a strong concern for perfection in this world tended to produce an achievement orientation in their sons, which turned the boys to business. Fifty years after revival,

England reached a peak of achievement as these men entered national and business leadership.[8]

Perhaps our primary political activity, then, is renewal at the grassroots. As we establish movements of men and women converted and passionately committed to holiness, they will act like leaven in bread and ultimately transform society.

Second, the assumption that the center of power is the Prime Minister or the President is based on a non-Christian concept of power. Establishing spiritual "power bases" among the poor may be the key to changing a society. Spiritual power, as opposed to political power, is used by people able to influence the One who rules over politicians.[9] Power to move the hand that moves the world can be tapped by poor Christians who know the scriptural injunction: "I urge that supplications, prayers, intercessions, and thanksgivings be made for all men, for kings and all who are in high positions, that we may lead a quiet and peaceable life, godly and respectful in every way" (1 Timothy 2:1–2).

Such prayers are not intoned set phrases repeated at weekly worship in dead churches. They are the prayers of people who know how to prevail on God to implement political change, who recognize that "The king's heart is a stream of water in the hand of the Lord; he turns it wherever he will" (Proverbs 21:1).

Righteous poor people who possess spiritual power and renounce natural concepts of power are, perhaps, the key to social change. But they must also be wise in the issues of the time. Poor but wise people, unable to be bought by wealth or power, are the key to godly societies.

St. Francis Xavier, the nobleman who renounced social status and opened Asia to the gospel, was one such poor, wise man. He won to Christ tens of thousands in India, the Moluccas, and Japan. He washed the wounds of lepers, prayed for the sick to be healed, and preached the gospel. Xavier sagely commented: "The world is not ruled by principles of politics or economics, but by the mysterious realities of sin and grace."[10]

Third, we work with the poor rather than the rich because of the example of Jesus. He could have come as a rich man—as the great welfare king. Instead, he came as a babe in a Bethlehem manger, surrounded by common shepherds.

He had a reason, though we don't fully understand it, to identify with and minister among the poor. He had a reason for refusing Herod's courts and Satan's offer.

For Jesus, doing justice involved riding not on a centurion's chariot, but on an ass. The heroes of his stories were children and slaves, not generals and politicians. Instead of overthrowing the unjust Romans and their empire (72,000 angels are a match for most Roman legions), he stopped to heal an ear with his touch.

But there will come a day when he will return with sword in hand, when the grapes of wrath will be pressed out and judgment on oppression, evil, and sin will be executed: "He will not fail or be discouraged till he has established justice in the earth" (Isaiah 42:4).

Jesus is a model of a revolutionary who never revolted, a man of power who refused others' concepts of power, a man of justice who refused to be others' judge, a man with his spirit attuned to the heavens who was constantly involved in dust and dirt, pain and people.[11]

Part of Jesus' genius in working with the poor was that the rich came to him as well. Nicodemus searched out Jesus because of Jesus' credentials. It was not Jesus' political power that attracted him. It was his observation of Jesus' spiritual power worked out in signs among the poor.

"Rabbi," he said, "we know that you are a teacher come from God; for no one can do these signs that you do, unless God is with him" (John 3:2).

In the same way, living among the poor of Manila gives credibility and an opening to the upper-class, for many upper-class Filipinos have a highly developed social conscience and are actively involved in helping the poor of their country.

Rothie was such a man: a politician, an academic, a former revolutionary, a man of integrity and compassion. During the Indonesian communist uprising, Rothie and a friend had flown to Indonesia to fight for justice. Later, as the executive assistant of a university, he had worked to clean up its corruption. This resulted in 117 staff being fired by presidential order—only to be reinstated when Libya put "oil" pressure on those in political power! Rothie left quickly after the reinstatement and for a year was afraid to leave his house.

But that didn't stop him. He began to work with local fishermen, seeking to break the cycle of poverty in which they lived. First he provided a punt boat which enabled their canoes to travel further out to sea, reap bigger catches, and extend their fishing season because of greater safety during the monsoon. He then studied how to better market their fish. He established a "cool" store, so the fish could be sold when the price was highest. Next he helped the fishermen's wives to become productive with gardening, goats, and sewing.

I met Rothie after he had come to a personal knowledge of Jesus Christ. From the moment I met him, I loved him. He was a man who sought after justice with all his heart—both in society and in his own life.

When he was an executive in the university, he organized a great feast for visiting Arab dignitaries. Rothie made sure all was in order and everybody adequately fed, and then he and his wife quietly stepped out the back door to their own room and ate canned sardines and rice.

One day, after he flew home from a meeting with government leaders about rights for a minority group, he told me, "I have cleared my calendar. I have three days. I want you to teach me the Scriptures."

This was a deeply humbling experience for a young, insecure, poorly taught missionary. My mind raced. What could *I* teach this brilliant anthropologist-politician? The only basis of rapport I had with such a man was that I cared enough about his people, the poor, to live with them. Suddenly, I thought of the contrast between God's political perspective and society's.

"We will work through the book of Daniel," I told him. "I think it will help you see God's ways of bringing about political change."

The loyal reformers

The Lord has opened doors for other upper-class Christians in Manila working to bring justice for the poor within the structures of government. They speak prophetically to the government and speak out against sin at all levels in society—personally and politically, from their positions of respect and honor. They take seriously our mandate to "pay . . . respect to whom respect is due, honor to whom honor is due" (Romans 13:7) and to "honor all men. Love the brotherhood. Fear God. Honor the emperor" (1 Peter 2:17)—even if he has no clothes!

These passages were written in the context of the great exploitation, oppression, and Machiavellian politics of the Roman Empire, so they hold true for us today no matter how evil a leadership rules over us.

Another example of a man with an *entree* to the seat of power was a colonel, an advisor to the President, whose task was to prepare plans for a sugar factory complex. After his conversion, he consumed book after book on the Christian basis for socio-political and economic development. He thought through a Christian framework as a basis for management-labor relations and profit sharing. His proposals were the basis for discussion at the highest level of government, discussion that inevitably included aspects of the gospel.

A host of biblical concepts on work, justice, and love are basic to labor relations. Take one statement to employers: "You shall not oppress a hired servant who is poor and needy, whether he is one of your brethren or one of the sojourners who are in your land within your towns" (Deuteronomy 24:14).

This brief statement would radically reform a large percentage of the factories and close some multinationals in Manila if it were applied today. The Bible is a never-to-be-put-down textbook on such issues as labor, profit making, work, successful management patterns, and many other areas of business and politics. The Bible clearly points out the responsibilities expected of people in high positions towards the poor.

While not in agreement with the major themes of Gustavo Gutierrez, I do appreciate his excellent summary of the biblical perspective:

> The Bible speaks of positive and concrete measures to prevent poverty from becoming established among the people of God. In Leviticus and Deuteronomy, there is very detailed legislation designed to prevent the accumulation of wealth and the consequent exploitation.
>
> It is said, for example, that what remains in the fields after the harvest and the gathering of olives and grapes should not be collected; it is for the alien, the orphan, the widow (Deut. 24:19–21; Lev. 19:9, 10). Even more, the fields should not be harvested to the very edge so that something remains for the poor and the aliens (Lev. 23:22).
>
> The Sabbath, the day of the Lord, has a social significance; it is a day of rest for the slave and the alien (Ex. 23:12; Deut. 5:14). The triennial tithe is

> not to be carried to the temple; rather it is for the
> alien, the orphan and the widow (Deut. 14:28–29;
> 26:12). Interest on loans is forbidden (Ex. 22:25; Lev.
> 25:35–37; Deut. 23:20). Other important measures
> include the Sabbath year and the jubilee year. Every
> seven years, the fields will be left to lie fallow "to
> provide food for the poor of your people" (Ex. 23:11;
> Lev. 25:2–7), although it is recognized that this duty
> is not always fulfilled (Lev. 26:34, 35). After seven
> years, the slaves were to regain their freedom (Ex.
> 21:2–6), and debts were to be pardoned (Deut.
> 15:1–18).

> This is also the meaning of the jubilee year of Lev.
> 25:10 ff. It was . . . a general emancipation . . . of
> all the inhabitants of the land. The fields lay fallow;
> every man reentered his ancestral property, i.e. the
> fields and houses which had been alienated returned
> to their original owners.[12]

It is difficult to function at upper levels of leadership within
a corrupt society. The higher up the ladder, the greater the extent
of corruption. In an oppressive regime, it is not unusual for a
Christian to reach a high level in government or business, only to
have to resign because of injustice.

The more corrupt a society's leaders become, the less
Christians are free to function. The church then moves more and
more into an Anabaptist, separatist lifestyle. Theologies based on
those of Calvin and Luther become less effective. Their theologies
came out of contexts where Christians had freedom to play a role
at the upper levels of society.

It is interesting to see this principle work out in the roles of the
prophets. The pre-exilic prophets in the Old Testament (Amos,
Hosea, Micah, Isaiah, and Jeremiah) worked from outside the
establishment, perhaps because of the extent of its evil, whereas
the post-exilic prophets (Joel, Haggai, Zechariah, and Malachi)

worked from within the established political and religious leadership. Emerging Christian leaders in developing countries today face a situation more akin to the pre-exilic one.

Demonic politics

Like the pre-exilic prophets, upper class Christians can "respect the Emperor" while standing in political opposition. Some, like Daniel, recognize the spiritual powers that function behind governments. One of the chief angels took three weeks to break out of a battle with the "prince of the kingdom of Persia" and reach Daniel. This supernatural being delayed him until finally Michael came to relieve him (Daniel 10:13).

Most politicians are people of the world, people who live outside of the Word of God. But some in power have been overcome not only by sin, but also by demonic principalities and powers. We readily recognize this in Hitler (even a cursory reading of his life shows all the classic symptoms of demonic possession), in Idi Amin, or in Colonel Gadaffi. Structures that such men create are not only corrupted by the world, as are all structures to some degree, but may be demonized.

It is against such "principalities [and] powers, against the world rulers of this present darkness, against the spiritual hosts of wickedness in the heavenly places" that we are to wrestle when entering the political realm. That is why prayer is our most potent political weapon. In Chapter 2 of Colossians, Paul tells us that the elemental spirits of the universe perpetrate both human philosophies and empty religious traditions. He reminds the Colossians that such "principalities and powers" are disarmed (rendered inoperative) by the cross.[13]

As workers in the slums seeking to bring justice, we are in direct confrontation with powerful demonic forces. How do we best confront such demons? Through love and reconciliation. While rejecting the demonic philosophies, we honor and respect all men. We work side by side with people who reject our faith, recognizing the genuine searchings of the social worker and the good intentions of the religious leader.

John Perkins sums up his own experience in a paragraph, which in many ways is the crux of his book, *With Justice for All:*

> Demanding our rights had not softened the white community as we hoped it would. Instead, it had stiffened their opposition. Lying there on my bed, I was able to see that confronting white people with hostility was only going to create war. If there was going to be any healing it would have to take place in an atmosphere of love. I had been trying to demand justice. Now God was opening my eyes to a new and better strategy—seeking reconciliation.
>
> I could not bring justice for other people. As a Christian, my responsibility was to seek to be reconciled. Then out of reconciliation, justice would flow.
>
> Affirmative action integration and so on might be useful, but they alone were not justice. True justice could come only as people's hearts were made right with God and God's love motivated them to be reconciled to each other.[14]

Contention with authorities

Defending the right and contending for truth are part of our call to righteousness. Jesus was no spineless coward. When slapped on the face and treated unjustly, he demanded, "Why do you strike me?" (John 18:23).

When the Pharisees misused their authority—an authority given by men but not by God—he refused to recognize it.

"You brood of vipers" is not a statement of a politician trying to win votes by compromise. It was the statement of the rightful King who had come to establish his kingdom.

The Old Testament prophets were not weak in their opposition to evil. Time and time again, God's spokesmen in the Scriptures recognized that he had appointed human authorities. They speak forcefully against sin. They do cry out in defense of cultural identity, and frequently call those in authority to repent. But they never call those under authority to rise up in rebellion.[15]

Moses, while leading a minority group out from oppression, went to the Pharaohs to gain permission and ultimately left the outcome to God. David, while outlawed from his society, refused to fight his king, leaving it to God to judge his case. Jude tells us that even when the archangel Michael contended with the devil, he said, "The Lord rebuke you." He did not presume to pronounce a reviling judgment himself.

But submission, gentleness, and obedience to authority are not humble acquiescence to unjust structures and unjust authority. Giving "honor to those whom honor is due" is not in conflict with contending for truth or standing for the rights of the poor. Love, honor, and reconciliation define the context and attitudes behind contention.

Ezekiel 45:9 has two interesting couplets: "Put away *violence and oppression,* and execute *justice and righteousness."*

Violence and oppression are linked together as the opposite of justice and righteousness. Some encourage violent revolution as a way of overcoming oppression. But righteousness and justice— not violence and bitterness—are the vanquishers of oppression.

Time and change

Why do we reject revolutionary violence? Those who would advocate it believe that gradual reforms of society are too slow, that political structures are too evil. By escalating the bitterness and bloodletting, the evil will be destroyed by *sudden change.*

Others champion *managed change,* recognizing that violent change unleashes forces into a community that destroy its fabric for generations.[16]

Christians recognize both components of change. Our action is to preach repentance—introducing reform step-by-step into a society to keep it from going rotten. But as we repent, we must recognize that some societies and structures within society (such as white slavery) are so evil that God will violently destroy them.

He does not desire increasing violence, but ends injustice through leaders who bring national repentance and transformation. Failing to find such people, God intervenes by his own arm. Such was the case of Nineveh in Jonah's day. Because the world's greatest city of its time repented, God did not destroy it!

Gradual reforms and revolutions may improve the lot of the poor. But we are not optimistic that they will create lasting "shalom." Christian reforms keep society from rottenness, but we must recognize our inability to make it holy.

Reforms are not reform enough. Revolutions are not revolutionary enough. But God's strategy is a long-term strategy that cannot fail. His kingdom, like a grain of mustard seed, will continue to grow until it has branches in every nation, tribe, and tongue. It advances through suffering servants who by the death of their Master overcome death, and who by the goodness of their lives disarm evil, hatred, and violence.

This is the good news, the hope that we proclaim day after day.

Political options

The chart on pages 196–197 summarizes possible Christian responses to the injustices of squatter society. There are three main categories of response. The first category is a "spiritual discipleship" model growing from Anabaptist, fundamentalist, or Pentecostal roots. These models encourage us to be "like Jesus."

The second category, the holistic discipleship model, is developed from a desire to see the kingdom rule *over* or be expressed *in* every facet of human life. It recognizes that Jesus chose to limit himself—to a single human body, to a time, to a people, to a geography, to a three-year ministry. The role he chose was and is today the spearhead of establishing the kingdom. But there are many other roles in the body of Christ.

This category considers kingdom *principles* to be eternal, but *applications* to be time and culture-bound. A Christian should not stay out of law as a career because Jesus was not a lawyer. There is a place for the Christian community development worker even though Jesus was not a community development worker. Because he was not a politician does not imply Christians should give up politics.

All of the Scriptures written across 2000 years need to be known and understood if we would know what is right to do in any given time and place. The Bible can help us be a godly lawyer, community developer, or politician. The principles lived out and taught by Jesus were also lived out by Moses the lawyer, Nehemiah the community developer, and Daniel the politician.

One difference between the first two categories is the understanding of power. Category I sees that since we are fighting against demonic forces and philosophies in government, we must rely primarily on spiritual warfare.

For "the weapons of our warfare are not physical [weapons of flesh and blood] but they are mighty before God for the overthrow and destruction of strongholds" (2 Corinthians 10:4, Amplified). Category I sees the power of God to heal the sick and set people free from demons as the spearhead of the kingdom of God.

Category II relates to those already in positions of political or economic power who need to learn the ethical uses of and

1. "Spiritual" discipleship model

Involvement	Historical Expressions	Focus of Energy
Non-involvement in politics	Under oppressive regimes (authorities controlled by demonic forces)	Alternative communities demonstrating kingdom power in non-violence
Involvement with the needy	Early church monastic orders	Ministry to the poor and needy
"Spiritual" power struggles (the suffering Christ)	Fundamentalists Mennonites Anabaptists	Conflict with demonic forces in heavenly places

2. Holistic discipleship model

Involvement	Historical Expressions	Focus of Energy
Alternative A:		
Political involvement, confrontation, and reform of the power structures (Christ the Reformer)	Under democracies Luther's attempts at an ordered society Franciscans	Reforming structures: Establishment of governments "infiltrated" with kingdom ethics
Alternative B:		
Involvement in structures with the ethically-based use of force or power (Christ the King)	The Salvation Army Tonga Calvin's Geneva	Controlling structures: Establishment of governments ruled by kingdom ethics

3. Christian deviations (non-Christian models—Christian language)

Involvement	Historical Expressions	Focus of Energy
Alternative A:		Accept structures
Abuse of power in the name of Christ (the "Byzantine Christ" of purple and scepter)	Christianized and post-Christian societies that have lost the moral base of legitimate power (Cromwell Post-Constantine era)	Establishment of kingdom of God on earth by force Kingdom of God seen as servant of political structures
Alternative B:		Overthrown structures
Use of power against secular authorities	Oppressive regimes	God's kingdom = revolutionary government
Power struggle with oppressive regimes (Christ the Zealot, Christ the humanitarian)	"Pax Marx" Liberation theology	Identification of the "principalities and powers" with corrupt political structures

1. "Spiritual" discipleship model (continued)

Involvement	Response to Violence	Political Action
Non-involvement in politics	Quietist approach	Submit to and pray for those in authority;
Involvement with the needy	Non-resistance	Proclaim gospel to the world; separate from evils of State
"Spiritual" power struggles		Overcome violence with pacifism

2. Holistic discipleship model (continued)

Involvement	Response to Violence	Political Action
Alternative A:		Individual participation
Political involvement, confrontation, and reform of the power structures	Activist approach Non-Violence	Use godly power (parents, reachers, etc.); rule justly; promote good legislation; be active in public office
Alternative B:		Prophetic proclamation
Involvement in structures with the ethically-based use of force or power	Establishment approach Violence or revolutionary violence	Organize petitions and boycotts; promote "biblical" civil disobedience; protest by using constitutional rights Civil defense

3. Christian deviations (continued)

Involvement	Response to Violence	Political Action
Alternative A:		
Abuse of power in the name of Christ	Just war Suppress dissent for piety and stability	Participation in exercise of amoral power, unjust rule, and institutional evil
Alternative B:		
Use of power against secular authorities	Combat violence with violence	Protest of evil = unrequited bitterness; Gospel of the Kingdom = gospel of revolution;
Power struggle with oppressive regimes		Establish alternative revolutionary structure; rebel against corrupt authorities; God is dead, so man must destroy evil

limitations of such power. Some may demonstrate, others pray, while others believe that proclaiming the Word of God to the politicians is more effective.

Category III includes non-biblical alternatives that advocate political viewpoints which themselves are not submitted to biblical authority.

Squatter politics

How does a worker in the slums practically pursue justice at the personal level, in peacemaking, in establishing communities of people, and in causing change at the upper levels of society? There are several key points to keep in mind as we seek to see God's justice come into slums and squatter settlements of the Two-Thirds World.

1. Living among the poor is itself seen as a political action. It is interpreted by many as a symbol of siding with the poor against the oppression of the rich (the government consisting of the rich).

2. Establishing churches where people care for each other and treat each other justly is itself a deeply political action. This involves proclamation, bringing reconciliation into families and between gangs, developing social activities and a social structure for new believers, and becoming involved in economic development projects and leadership training. The worker must relate well to community leaders and government agency employees.

3. Public and private prayer for those in authority enables God to bring justice into society. It is a priority.

4. Since the national Intelligence Service may have a dossier on many Christian leaders, the Christian worker must be careful to clear activities with local leaders so that any questions might be answered beforehand, and all is above board. The worker

should avoid becoming aligned with any political faction in a community.

5. The Christian worker needs to treat community leaders with respect and become involved with them at a practical level. These relationships provide a basis for rebuke when they act corruptly or consultation when the community is threatened.

6. Healing the sick, casting out demons, and bringing about changes through prayer also pave the way for a prophetic ministry to community leaders.

7. The basic issue for illegal squatters is to gain land rights. The Christian worker can encourage oppressive landlords or government officials to repent. Similar confrontations may take place over housing programs, water rights, and sewerage.

8. Believers must first maintain right relationships at home, school, and the office. The Christian worker tries to bring conciliation between groups within the community, organizes protests against civil authorities through petitions and lobbying for land, employment, sewerage, and so on. The people in the community should be encouraged to see the social responsibilities they share, like policing crime, wiping out corruption, securing garbage disposal, and improving hygiene. They should cooperate with the government upgrading program if it is designed and implemented well.

9. The servant of God is not called to handle all these issues. Let me cite three areas of citywide injustice too big for any one person to handle.

In July 1982, Madame Imelda Marcos began a new anti-squatting drive. The "benevolent society" wished to clean up Manila, "the City of Man." Thousands of people were loaded into trucks and deposited into relocation sites miles from the city—without water, without work, without promised facilities.[16]

"Thus says the Lord God: Enough, O princes of Israel! Put away violence and oppression, and execute justice and righteousness; cease your evictions of my people, says the Lord GOD" (Ezekiel 45:9). No one person could stop this oppression alone.

The slave trade can only occur because the uppermost level of government protects it. Who dares take it on alone?[17]

What about the exportation of Filipino laborers to the Middle East? This is a big source of steady income for family left behind in the squatter settlement, but it has led to thousands of situations of exploitation and trickery. Christian models of recruiting agencies need to be set up. Christian legislation needs to be introduced. Again, who can do this alone?

We need to see ourselves as part of the whole body of Christ and work in partnership to address these larger issues of injustice.

Unattached!

I read Malcolm Muggeridge's book *Something Beautiful for God* on the life of Mother Teresa, and found that while not neglecting programs, she had concluded that the greatest gift is loving people, communicating to them their dignity and their worth, even when there is no final way to meet their physical needs. Transferring the personal love and power of God is ultimately of infinite and eternal value.

Involvement with the poor results in different activities and responses in every community, for each community's needs differ. While we may not solve the problems facing squatters, we must do all in our power to alleviate them.

And we can dream. But we hold lightly our dreams for the cities of the world, because our eyes are fixed on an eternal city designed and built by God. Although unattached to this present world, we freely serve it, for love and justice compel us to. We work with all the energy he inspires within us to preach his kingdom and carve it into the structures of society here on earth.

When the King returns, that kingdom of justice and righteousness will be fully established. The end of those who oppress others and show contempt for God will come (Isaiah 29:20). This vision of the holy city keeps us going in the midst of suffering and sorrow. Even so, come quickly Lord Jesus.

Coming full circle

Milleth had just taught us a Jewish dance. Everybody was rejoicing. The late afternoon shadows rustled back and forth in the wind. Sito announced our special guest—Aling Nena!

She stood up in her finest dress. She had just had her teeth removed and smiled in embarrassment. Then, in clear Tagalog, she began her story.

"I used to be a gambler and a drunkard," she told us. "Now my life is changed. It is Jesus who has done this!"

Although most of us knew her story, we listened in silence.

She continued, "What I want to do now is to go to those poor people who live on the rubbish dump and preach to them about Jesus. They are poorer than we are. I want them to know what Jesus can do!" And so the kingdom spreads.

NOTES
1. See also Waldron Scott, *Bring Forth Justice* (Authentic Media, 1997), 64–67.
2. Jose Porfirio Miranda, *Marx and the Bible,* trans. John Eagleson (Wipf & Stock Publishers, 2004), 93.
3. In his book *Beyond Manila,* Castillo provides a well-researched analysis of the structural causes and effects of Philippine rural poverty—which is the major cause of urban poverty. Celia T. Castillo. *Beyond Manila, Philippine Rural Problems in Perspective,* International Development Research Center, Box 8500, Ottawa, Canada K1G 3H9, 1980.
4. John Perkins, *With Justice for All* (Regal Books, 1982), 105. Used by permission.
5. Donald Dumbaugh, "Is 'Withdrawal' Involvement?", *The Other Side,* Box 158, Savannah, Ohio 44874, March-April 1974, pp 21–23.

6. Alan R. Tippett. *People Movements in Southern Polynesia* (Moody Press, 1971).

7. Ian Bradley, "Saints against Sin," reprinted from the Observer in *The Other Side,* March-April. 1974, pp 24–27.

8. McLelland, "Business Drive and National Achievement", in *Social Change: Sources, Patterns and Consequences* (Basic Books, 1973), 171 ff.

9. For a theological analysis of the problem of power see Martin Hengel, "Christ and Power", trans. by Everett R. Kalin, *Christian Journals,* (Ireland) Ltd, 1977. The diverse perspectives are analysed by Tom McAlpine, *Facing the Powers: What are the Options?* (Monrovia: MARC, 1991).

10. Xavier Leon Dujour S.J. *Saint Francis Xavier, The Mystical Progress of the Apostle,* Fr. Henry Pascual Diz, S.J., (Bandra, Bombay: St. Paul Press Training School, 1950).

11. For a broader discussion of Jesus' rejection of revolution see John H. Yoder, *The Original Revolution* (Scottdale, PA: Herald Press, 1971), and Ronald Sider, *Christ and Violence* (Wipf & Stock Publishers, 2001).

12. Gustavo Gutierrez, *A Theology of Liberation,* 15th edition, Sr. Caridad Inda and John Eagleson, trans, and eds. Maryknoll, (Orbis Books, 1988).

13. See Henrik Berkhof, *Christ and the Powers,* trans. John H. Yoder, (Herald Press, 1962, 1977), for a theological analysis of the demonic in politics.

14. Perkins, John, ibid, p. 102. Used by permission.

15. Leon Morris, "The Responsible Make Legends Happen," *Christianity Today,* September 7, 1979.

16. *Wretched of the Earth,* Concerned Citizens for the Urban Poor, Series 2, and Danilo-Luis M. Manano, *The Last Campaign,* Observer, Manila, 19 September 1982.

17. Spencer Davidson and David De Voss, *Lust City in the Far East* (Time May 10, 1982), or for fuller analyses Ron O'Grady *Third World Stopover* (WCC, 1981), and F. Landa Jocano, *Slums as a Way of Life* (University of the Philippines Press, 1975), chapter IX.

Chapter Twelve

Whom Will I Send?

A VISION FOR SERVING ASIA'S URBAN POOR

Verses from Ecclesiastes came to mind one evening when I was back in New Zealand.

> There was a little city with a few men in it;
> and a great king came against it and besieged it,
> building great siegeworks against it.
> But there was found in it a poor, wise man,
> and he by his wisdom delivered the city.
> Yet no one remembered that poor man.
> But I say that wisdom is better than might,
> though the poor man's wisdom is despised,
> and his words are not heeded
> (Ecclesiastes 9:14–16).

Battered by reverse culture shock, by illness, and by the rejection of friends, I was wandering down a bush track in the evening light. As I prayed, God brought a picture to my mind—a brilliant picture, in a manner I've come to recognize as from God.

He showed me a hundred "poor, wise" men and women wandering the byways of the slums, dwelling among the poor of ten great cities in Asia—men and women who would, as Wesley says, "fear nothing but God and hate nothing but sin."

A few days later, an artist living up the road dropped me a note with a message the Lord had given her. It spoke of the same call to establish a new movement.

For months I delayed, praying, *Lord, I have no contacts with the influential men of the church. Why call me to establish a movement? Physically, I feel sick! Emotionally, I am in shock! Socially, I have lost my friends!*

But the Lord continued to encourage me. I decided not to visit the influential people, but to start where I was, take what I had, and do what I could. I visited some friends. As I began to speak of the need in the slums, the Spirit of God was evident in unusual ways.

Wherever I went, I found renewal—renewal that would break out when proud Christian leaders had humbled themselves before God. People would take me to meet these leaders. Most would listen humbly to this unknown missionary, and then confirm that indeed this was God's voice, and he would raise up this work.

God had already spoken to many others about the poor of Asia's cities. He had prepared the way, and a new missionary movement began.

Wanted: rugged laborers

My message to these churches was simple. God's method is people!

Do we not hear a call to go as servants of that rugged cross, laborers whose delight is work, sacrifice and suffering, whose souls are filled with compassion, and whose lifestyle is that of simple poverty?

In the next few years, there needs to be an ever-growing stream, a new thrust to these dirt-and-plywood jungles. We need bands of people who, on fire with the message of Christ's kingdom, will choose a *lifestyle of simplicity* to proclaim that kingdom to the *poorest of the poor*.

These bands can include people at different life stages or of different marital status, but primarily include men and women who deliberately choose singleness for a period, couples without children, or couples whose children have grown up. Together they will form "cells" or "communities" of six to ten workers to go to each of these great cities.

These teams need to be trained in the sending country. When they arrive in the host city, they will begin a full year of language study and continued orientation. During this time, these teams will be split up, going two-by-two to different squatter areas. One day a week, they will gather together for relaxation, mutual ministry, further training, and celebration of the Lord's Supper at a retreat center, led by an older, mature couple with pastoral and administrative oversight for the "community."

We need men and women willing to commit themselves to this task initially for six years—this being long enough to establish a first church—but with the *intention* of spending fifteen to twenty years in the urban community to establish a discipling movement.

It is not unreasonable for a young person to trust that God will bring fruit during these fifteen to twenty years. Is it a big enough request to ask God for 1,500 new Christians—or 3,000 or 15,000? A harvest like that would be a worthy lifetime's work. Many have seen God do this elsewhere.

In 1898, Hudson Taylor, with the vast needs of inland China in mind, issued a call for "twenty able, earnest and healthy young men willing to consecrate five years of their lives to itinerant work, without thought of marriage or of settling down till their special work is accomplished." We need a similar breed of Christians for today's "new" mission field in the Asian mega-cities.

Younger couples may need to delay having children until they have had time to establish themselves in these slum communities, know how to cope with poverty, drunkenness, the food, the climate, hatred, and learn how to raise children in such an environment.

On each team, the gifts needed are infinite: a comic designer, an apostle-evangelist, an apostle-pastor team leader, an administrator, a poet-communicator, a specialist in establishing small-scale industries, etc. But above all, men and women with a drive, zeal, and training in the practice of establishing the Kingdom of God are needed: people who can preach and disciple; those who are able to consolidate small Bible studies and transform multitudes of believers into movements of disciples; men and women with eternity in their hearts, the promises of God in their souls, and the fire of holiness in their spirits; men and women of a rugged cross.

The apostle Peter was such a man. He walked in a poor man's wooden sandals (Acts 12:8) and had no gold for the beggar at the Temple (Acts 3:6).

Similarly, the apostle Paul underwent stonings, beatings, and shipwrecks, living "as poor, yet making many rich" (2 Corinthians 6:10) in his desire to reach the cities of his world.

Stories are told of Toribio, who traveled barefoot through Mexico. Other Mexicans called him "the poor one" because he was evidently poorer than they were. He learned the Aztec language quickly and preached fluently in that language. The Indians loved him like a father and regarded him almost like a divine Inca because of his total commitment and absolute poverty. He covered 40,000 miles on foot. He had nothing of his own to leave behind when he died.

Above all, we need to remember the Master, who calls us to walk in his sandaled footsteps. He chose poverty in birth, poverty in life and finally, blood dripping from thorn-crowned brow, chose poverty on the cross of a criminal.

Who will go? Who will take up the cross and follow him?

Who will give fifteen or twenty years for the poorest of the people in the slums of Asia? Who will live among them, love them, and show them the King? Is this such an unreasonable request from the Lord who gave his all?

Renewal

As I visited churches calling for these "rugged laborers," God was going before me, bringing renewal.

There seemed to be three phases of renewal. The first was a phase of brokenness, humbling, repentance, restitution, and seeking the Lord. In this phase, God broke into people's lives in a new way with power, resulting in worship, evangelism, and the exercise of spiritual gifts.

The second phase was a restructuring of traditional church life. House groups developed. Deep relationships and spiritual ministry to inner personal need occurred. Evangelism, flowing through normal social relationships, multiplied new believers. Where there was strong leadership training and disciplined intake of the Word of God, economic changes and care for the poor became part of a new pattern of life.

Four or five years after renewal of an older church or the birth of a new fellowship, a third phase emerged. Scores of people developed an eagerness to be involved in missions. Hundreds upon hundreds volunteered for the field.

My role was to walk behind the movement, sensing what God was doing, and providing a structure to facilitate this missions thrust. We formed a new mission structure called "Urban Leadership Foundation" to accommodate the people who wanted to serve Asia's urban poor.

No unemployment

The vision I had seen called for a hundred laborers. A hundred laborers means a hundred church-planters—people who can pioneer new fellowships in unreached areas. Such a task requires all the social, intellectual, and spiritual capacities a person has. No lifestyle can match the thrill of church-planting. None demands so much from a person.

Renewal alone will not produce such men and women. It takes eight or nine years of mature training in a dynamic church situation to produce a leader ready to serve in Asia. If we would develop long-term cross-cultural missionaries, the critical element is an *apprenticeship relationship.*

Elisha, apprentice to Elijah, received a double portion of Elijah's spirit. Joshua, forty years' servant of Moses, led the people into Israel. Paul could say of Timothy: "I have no one else like him, who is genuinely interested in your welfare."

In the past, training has been a unique contribution of a number of para-church organizations in the body of Christ. Churches need encouragement to develop this apprenticeship model of training laborers.

As God called more men and women to work among the poor, I would sit down with the pastor and elders of a church and discuss with them principles and phases of training potential laborers. Pastors were excited to see a new pattern of ministry opening up before them. Theologically, they had moved to a commitment to training. They appreciated practical input that helped them implement this new theology.

In response, I adapted a "Focus Chart" that had been developed by Gene Tabor. My version came to be known as "The Four Seasons of Christian Training." Rather than giving an entire program of training as most groups do, this model gives training principles to use during the four commonly identifiable stages of growth of a potential worker. Pastors and elders would spend considerable time enthusiastically discussing what stages they were in and what the next steps of growth should be.

The first season is a healthy Christian "babyhood" in a warm, relational, celebrating home-group and church fellowship. Most growing churches had become skilled in providing this.

The second season requires more personal discipling of the person by an elder or house group leader in the context of ministering to a small group of other believers.

The third season is the involvement of disciples in ministry to others as part of the church's ministry team—as house-group leaders, youth leaders, part of the counseling or outreach team, and so on. Even the leader of a nursery can use this role to disciple young mothers. During this stage of growth, the critical element is development of character. Potential leaders need to meet at least fortnightly to minister to one another at the personal level, relating scriptural teaching to the problems or matters that have emerged during the past fortnight.

The fourth season of training focuses on developing gifts and calling. It can involve a semi-independent ministry; establishing a church or pioneering a new ministry thrust.

Robin and his merry men

There is another kind of laborer in the Scriptures—men and women skilled as deacons and deaconesses. We not only need the apostle, the pastor-teacher, and the evangelist; we need men and women filled with the Holy Spirit and with wisdom—men and women skilled in using money given by the rich to meet the needs of the poor. (The early deacons' biggest responsibility was not giving out hymnals at the door!)

We need people skilled in establishing small-scale industries: carpentry shops, electronic shops, and machine shops. We need men and women skilled in social work, administration, and community development. Couples in their forties and fifties whose children are now independent are the best possible people for such tasks.

Wisdom

In Ecclesiastes, the poor man who saved the city was wise. The wisdom needed to minister in the slums is not primarily learned in school. Christ imparted his wisdom in the context of loving action. His type of wisdom has to do with character, decision-making, ethical issues, and relationships.

Yet godly wisdom is not only acquired "on the street." As Solomon adds, wisdom is based on "getting knowledge, getting understanding." It has an intellectual component.

The urban mission field needs men and women of the finest academic training. The cultural understanding needed to mobilize a movement comes from the finest training in language learning, cross-cultural missions theory, and church history. Community development and church growth principles must be mastered if the kingdom will be established in a community. The complexity of issues is unending.

We must upgrade our schools to provide the best postgraduate evangelical training in such areas. If we find an un-biblical anti-intellectualism inherent in our churches (despite our penchant for academic degrees and titles), we must renounce it.

God's wisdom comes from the Spirit revealing the mind of Christ. Finely trained minds are the outworking of the gift of spiritual discernment. Workers need to have discernment concerning the leading of the Spirit. They need to know how to use spiritual gifts in confrontations with the demonic, in healing the sick, in prophecy, through a (supernatural) word of discernment, through a word of knowledge, or through the interpretation of dreams.

The missionary needs to be a person of balance—sound in theology, bold and authoritative, but meek and flexible; able to exercise spiritual gifts and power, but not extremist; fully developing his academic capacities, but deeply spiritual and pragmatic.

Urban workers need to be able to grapple with the concepts of the Scriptures. They will not teach using books and concepts, but, like their Master, using story and parable. The ability to tell stories grows out of a full life, marked by a fine sensitivity—an ability to feel what others around you are feeling. The urban missionary must be a leader in the midst of the people, able to incarnate a people's soul, speak their poetry, and understand their aspirations.

This is the gift of cross-cultural communication. It requires strength of will on the inside, an inner fiber coupled with above-average sensitivity, flexibility, and adaptability. It involves a capacity for suspended judgment—being able to hold two opposing views in one's mind without feeling buried by tension. The black-and-white absolutist or judgmental thinker is not a natural missionary.

Above all, urban missionaries need to be men and women of the Word of God. A layperson can do an in-depth study of all the Scriptures over five or six years and memorize several hundred passages that will transform thought patterns. The main goal of studying the Bible is to know, love, and understand Jesus. The values and actions he talks about in the Sermon on the Mount will best prepare us to cross cultures. Perhaps memorizing that sermon is the place to begin.

Missionary school

Along with theological and vocational education, training for such a man or woman is along the lines of the training Jesus gave the disciples—spending time with alcoholics, rescuing lesbians and homosexuals, walking for months with the drug addict, explaining the gospel to abusive students, living among the poorest immigrant community, healing prejudice, and visiting prisoners. The more difficult the sufferings encountered in our comfortable Western society, the better equipped the missionary will be.

Missionaries to the poor should study the lives of those who have walked before them: Hudson Taylor, Xavier, Assisi, or Mother Teresa, Amy Carmichael, Sadhu Sundar Singh, and so on.

They should grapple with the social implications of the gospel in their own country to have a basis for grappling with it elsewhere, picking up social work and community development skills where possible.

Learning to work under authority is important. Only those with the power of submission, those able to trust others with decisions about their lives will survive the tensions of a mission community. Such lessons must be learned *before* reaching the field.

Potential missionaries should be taught to live without possessions (except books, since these contribute to wisdom, and tools of the trade). They should learn to eat little meat and few desserts, to know how to keep their bodies healthy through wise diet, natural foods, the use of herbs and good exercise. They should practice living in crowded conditions and coping with constant pressures.

The urban missionary must be able to integrate a life that relates both to the poor as well as to the rich. In this way, the missionary to the slums will find life less comfortable than the missionary to a remote village. Village missionaries can resume their Western roles when they visit the city. But slum missionaries must continually balance an incarnational lifestyle against the need to build relationships with mentors and officials in universities and government agencies. They must wear several hats at the same time.

Francis Xavier was insistent on tested men for the mission field. He suggested the following tests for potential missionaries:

> The spiritual exercises will be made for a month, in order to judge the nature of the individual, his steadfastness, temperament, inclinations and vocation. For another month he will serve the poor in the hospitals in every kind of menial work he might be ordered to perform, because to humble oneself in all meekness and care nothing for the esteem of the

world is to set at naught human respect. During the third month, he must make a pilgrimage on foot and without money, placing his entire hope in the Creator and Lord, accustoming himself to bad food and a comfortless bed. He who cannot either rest or travel without food and with poor sleep for twenty-four hours will be unable, we believe, to persevere in the Society.[1]

It was not enough to Xavier that we have spiritual yearnings and romantic dreams. We need to pass tough tests before qualifying as workers among the poor. The harvest is urgent, but God takes time to train his harvesters.

Sacrifice

The call is costly in terms of family relationships, separation from children and health. "How lonesome the weary hours confined to my room," wrote Hudson Taylor upon the death of his wife. "How I missed my dear wife and the little pattering footsteps of the children far away in England." While God never calls us to desert our family responsibilities, he may, for a limited season, call us to sever those links.

Most great mission leaders, while knowing God's power in prayer for the sick, were often sickly themselves, living in difficult climates, in situations of poorly controlled hygiene.

All extension of the kingdom is accomplished at cost. Yet the Lord is not our debtor. Our children, our wives, our husbands, our bodies are his. He holds them in his hands and can do as he wills with them.

Kagawa wrote this poem to his wife:

> You who dwell
> in the heart of my heart
> Listen to me;
> This you must know—

I am a child of grief and pain
Bending my fingers to count my woe.
You yield me everything;
But I have nothing
I can bring
To give to you.
Know
You have married
Poverty, sorrow;
Bear it with me;
The storm will be over
Tomorrow.
A little while
For us
The rod;
And then,
Then God.[2]

His wife Haru had not only married a man who would always be wandering—she had married a life of poverty and sorrow.

For many, work in the slums is a call to celibacy; for others, a life of singleness for some years. This call to singleness is not a call to individualism, but to involvement in a community. Singleness in the ancient orders involved vows of chastity. A commitment to chastity, or purity of heart, is contrary to all the tendencies of nature. But chosen singleness is not a breaking of human affections. It is given that we might love our neighbor more fully. Singleness is a calling in God's economy, enabling people to more deeply know their Lord. Many people give their early years to the pursuit of love—we must give it to the pursuit of God.

A poor man

In Ecclesiastes, the wise man who saved cities was also poor. The missionary of today is one who can support himself and others using income earned through a trade or profession. Our choice of poverty is not a choice of dependency. Our poverty is chosen as a sign of love and justice. It is not to be a burden, but to bring joy! It will set free for it is freely chosen. "Laboring poverty" cannot be legislated by the rules of a mission. It is chosen freely by those who, having forsaken wealth, cannot be bought by money; having forsaken power, cannot be bought position and influence; having forsaken all security, cannot be bought by the offer of security.

Such a lifestyle and level of commitment is hard to maintain. Enthusiasm of the early days passes away; easier courses appear; the capacity to suffer often decreases as one suffers. Idealism easily dims, and in doing so, it may either bring balance or turn one back from earlier single-mindedness. And the constant glitter of the cities in which we dwell subtly brings captivity to the desire for things.

The Apostle Peter struggled, too. He once told Jesus, "Lord, we have left everything to follow you." What he really was asking was, "What do we get out of it?"

Jesus did not rebuke him. His reply was: "There is no one who has left house or brothers and sisters or mother or father or children or lands, for my sake and for the gospel, who will not receive a hundredfold now in this time, houses and brothers and sisters and mothers and children and lands, with persecutions, and in the age to come eternal life" (Mark 10:28–30).

The movement

Behind such a mission thrust of poor, wise men and women, we need a movement of hundreds of men and women in the sending base. These "senders" choose another sort of poverty—that of simplicity.

This is the commitment of my home church. They send and support almost thirty missionaries. The means of supporting these laborers? Simplicity!

One church leader has chosen to limit his engineering business to supply only his basic needs and devote himself to the business of the kingdom. Some have chosen homes half as expensive as they formerly owned. Others sit down and calculate every area of expense to see if they can spend less. They count each item in their possession, sell the excess items counted, and give to the poor. Many have given their best clothes to the poor. Some have sold their jewelry. One couple, in response to the Lord's prompting, gave a welding machine for the poor in the slums.

These are ordinary men and women, "living simply that others may simply live," living frugally that missionaries may continue spreading the kingdom, living without to win the fight against the demon of materialism that controls our nations. They live out their simplicity communally with other believers to battle the twin brother of materialism—excessive individualism. It has destroyed not only our society, but also our nuclear family structures. It is the cause of the new poverty of the urban West.

How can we live communally? In New Zealand, the most effective communal structure has been the house group, a weekly meeting of six to fifteen people learning to mold their lives together as "family," seeking to hear God's direction, worshipping, and studying the word together. Members struggle together with the social and economic implications of the kingdom. Sharing money, recreation, garden tools, meals, vehicles, and ministry all have emerged as natural outcomes.

Some have added semi-detached quarters to their home for a solo mother, widow, or single young folk. Others have obtained three or four houses close to each other in the same street to share the load of hospitality, child supervision, and possessions.

Along with such communities of committed believers, God longs to raise up a band of praying people who will give their lives to prayer for the slums. An older woman of eighty-four has prayed daily for me these thirteen years. A young woman has chosen to work half time and give her life to prayer. A band of women in my church are known as women of intercession. This is the pattern of history. Nunneries have been the source of power for numerous movements. Assisi and his men, in times of confusion and uncertainty, would repair to Saint Clara and her sisters and ask these cloistered women to seek the Lord's will on their behalf.

Servants of the Lord

Seventy of us were gathered in prayer, worshipping God. Seven had just been commissioned to Asia's slums. Others had committed themselves to training in preparation to go.

As we sang together, a picture of the Lord came to mind.

He came from Mount Zion on a magnificent white charger, descending upon one of the great cities of Asia. Millions of city-dwellers lined its streets, all worshipping God in song and dance. There seemed to be no rich, no poor. Each one had a home. But all had left their work and homes to worship the King.

By the city gates, in the middle of the crowd, was a wizened, simply garbed man leaning on his staff—not noticeably different from the crowd. But as the King swept through the gates, he paused, looked across the crowd, and greeted the servant with a smile, a nod, and a simple "well done."

The King continued on his way as the millions delighted with him. And the companion to the poor was content with his labor.

NOTES

1. Xavier Leon Du Jour, S.J., *St. Francis Xavier,* trans. Henry Pascual Oiz, S.J., (Bandra, Bombay: St. Paul Press Training School, 1950), 65–66.
2. Toyohiko Kagawa, "The Cross of the Whole Christ," in *Meditations on the Cross* (SCM, 1936).

Further Information

About Viv Grigg

God has used Viv Grigg in inspiring new movements to and among the squatter and slum areas of the Two-Thirds World.

While writing *Companion to the Poor,* Grigg and several other "Kiwis" founded a New Zealand-based mission called Servants to Asia's Urban Poor. Then, with Dr. Betty Sue Brewster and the late Dr. Tom Brewster, he led a mission called Servants to the Poor in the United States. With Pastor Waldemar Carvalho in Brazil, he catalyzed Servos Entre Os Pobres, which is now part of KAIROS mission.

Grigg then poneered work in a megacity behind the Hindu curtain, with his wife Iêda and their daughter Monique. Iêda was one of the first Brazilian missionaries to India and is a motivating communicator. This was followed by development of reconciliation community in a poor suburb of Los Angeles. While living there, he coordinated the Cities network of the AD2000 movement until 1996. He developed the Vision for Auckland network and has been chairing the Encarnação network of urban poor mission leaders. Together with these leaders, he is developing a training process on CD Rom and the web that takes stories from Africa, Asia, and Latin America and gets them to urban poor workers around the world.

Grigg is a graduate of Fuller School of World Missions, and is working on his doctorate in theology of transformative revival at Auckland University. Another book, *Cry of the Urban Poor,* an analysis of the worldwide need for churches in the slums and case studies in slum church planting is published by Authentic.

Currently, Grigg directs Urban Leadership Foundation, from which he initiated these and other ministries.

Involvement

Further information on work in Manila, Kolkuta, Sao Paulo, Bangkok, and other cities may be obtained from, or gifts for the Griggs' ministry may be designated for them and sent to:

Urban Leadership Foundation
P.O.Box 20-524,
Glen Eden,
Auckland, New Zealand
www.urbanleaders.org